Building Saint Tabitha's House

The Story of a Greek Orthodox Orphanage in Kenya

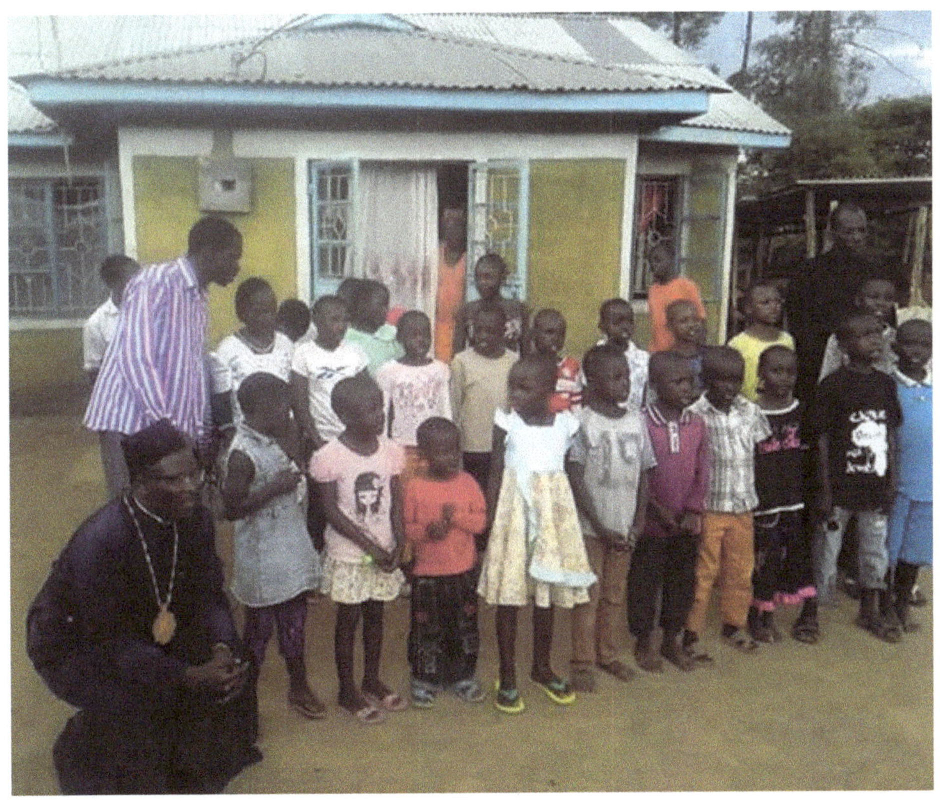

ISBN: 978-0-9941799-7-5

Publication year:	2018
Book Title:	Building Saint Tabitha's House
Language:	English
Publisher:	Michael Raymond Astle
Printer:	Ingram Spark
Location:	Melbourne, Australia
Author:	M. R. Astle & the children of Saint Tabitha's House
Binding:	Paperback
Target Audience:	Family
Subjects:	PHO015000 Photography : Photojournalism REL045000 Religion : Christian Ministry - Missions EDU020000 Education : Multicultural Education

Contents

Introduction

Saint Tabitha's House is built by ordinary men and women, boys and girls. Most of them were born in Kenya. Some of them send support from all over the world in different ways. A few visit.

This is a story told through the eyes of those who are there. It is mostly a photographic record of events which have shaped the history of a faithful community of people who have come together to support children in need. Throughout, there are comments explaining some of the happenings and significant people involved, the thoughts and feelings of the children, expressions of gratitude, and numerous letters of appeal from the children themselves. The letters were written in a hurry after a last minute request to include them. They were based upon a template given to the children but this does not detract from their sincerity in asking for your support too.

Our Family

At Saint Tabitha's House,
we are all one big family.

God is our Father in heaven and
we are all his children.

He gives us each day
our daily bread.

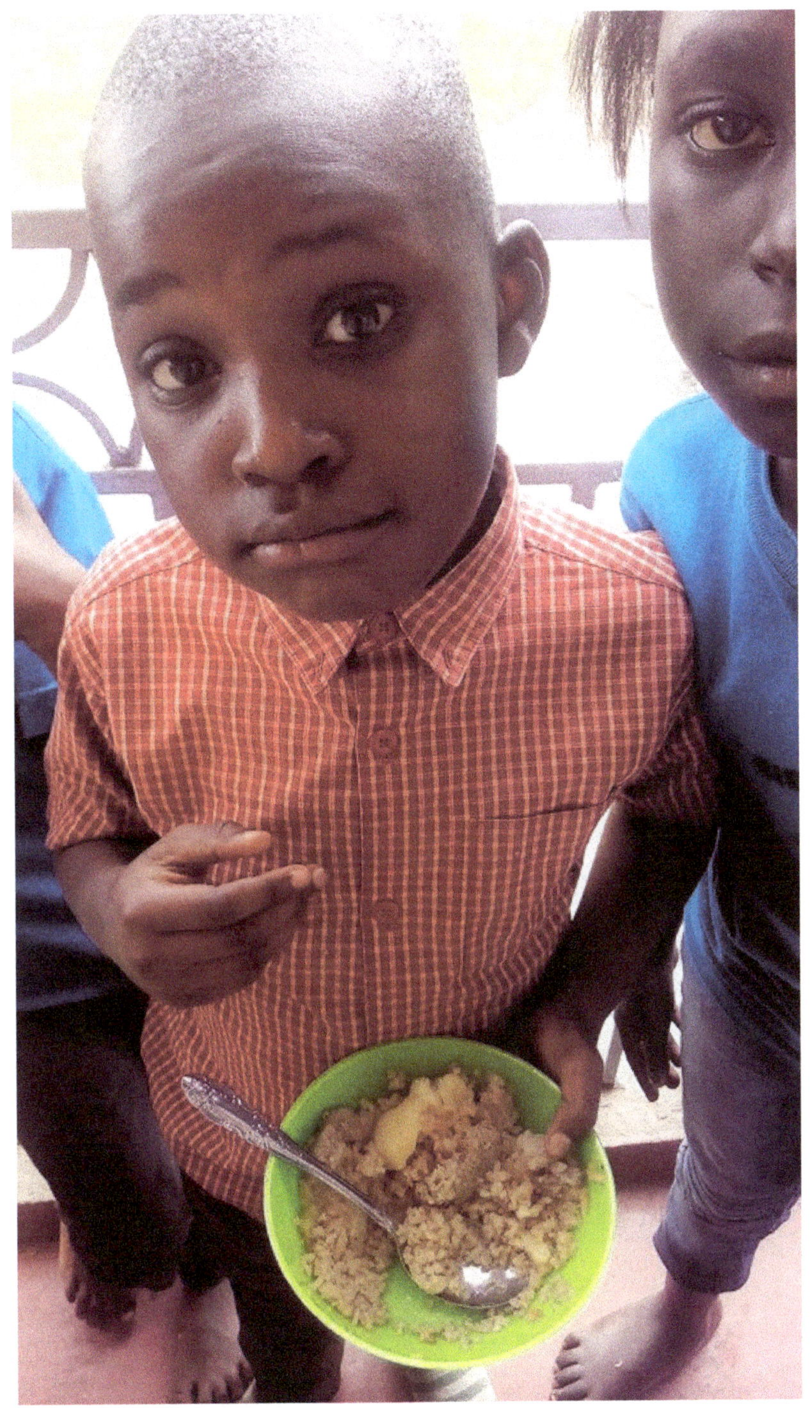

25/04/2018

Dear, friends;

Hello, my name Trevor Masolia 9 9 years old boy at St. Tabitha orthodox church and School in class 3.

I respect the people around me and wishing to go far in my education and become a pilot. Requesting you for more support. Thank you

Yours sincerely
Trevor Masolia

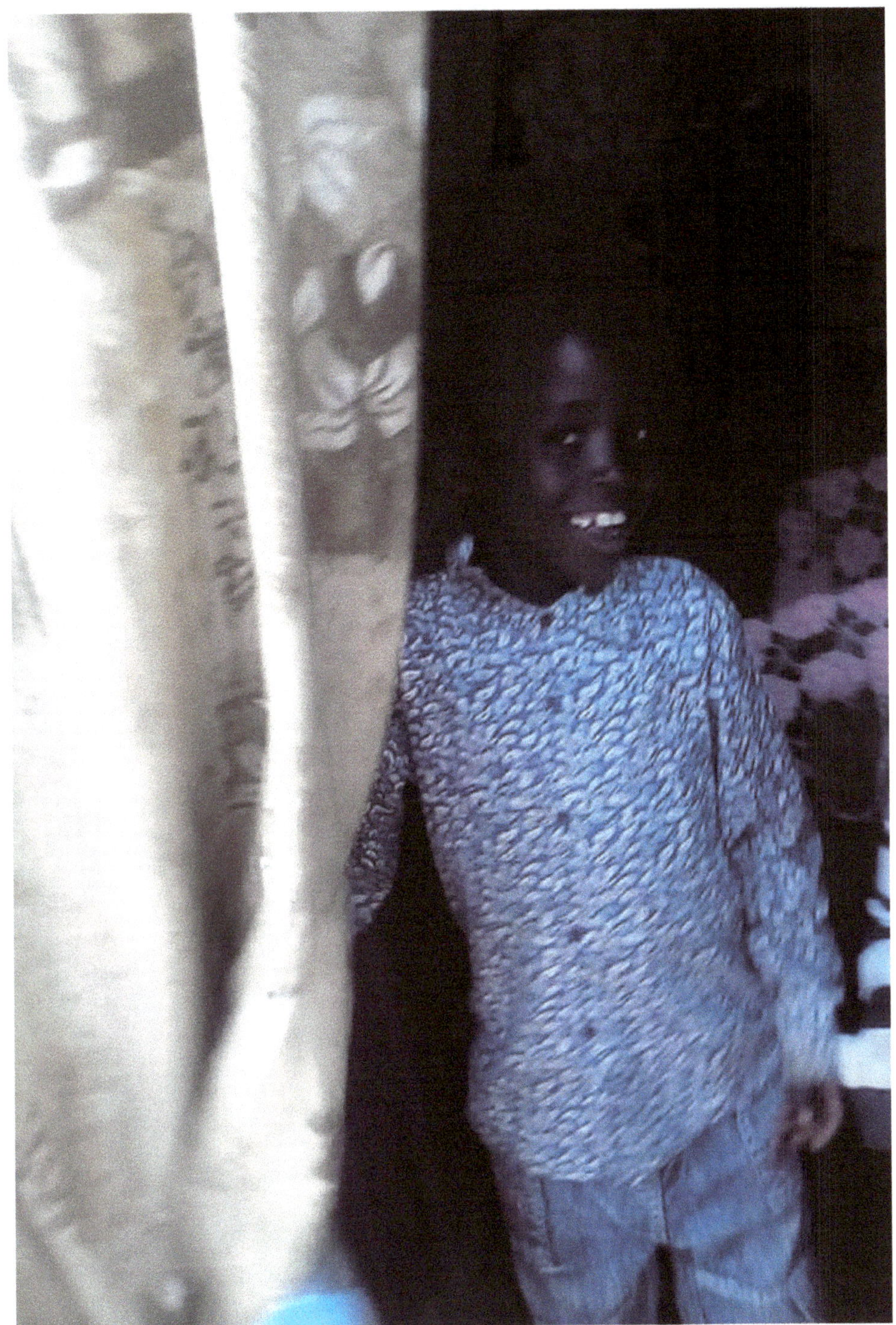

We had a view if we ate outside at our old location.

We always have more time to play before school if we finish eating breakfast quickly.

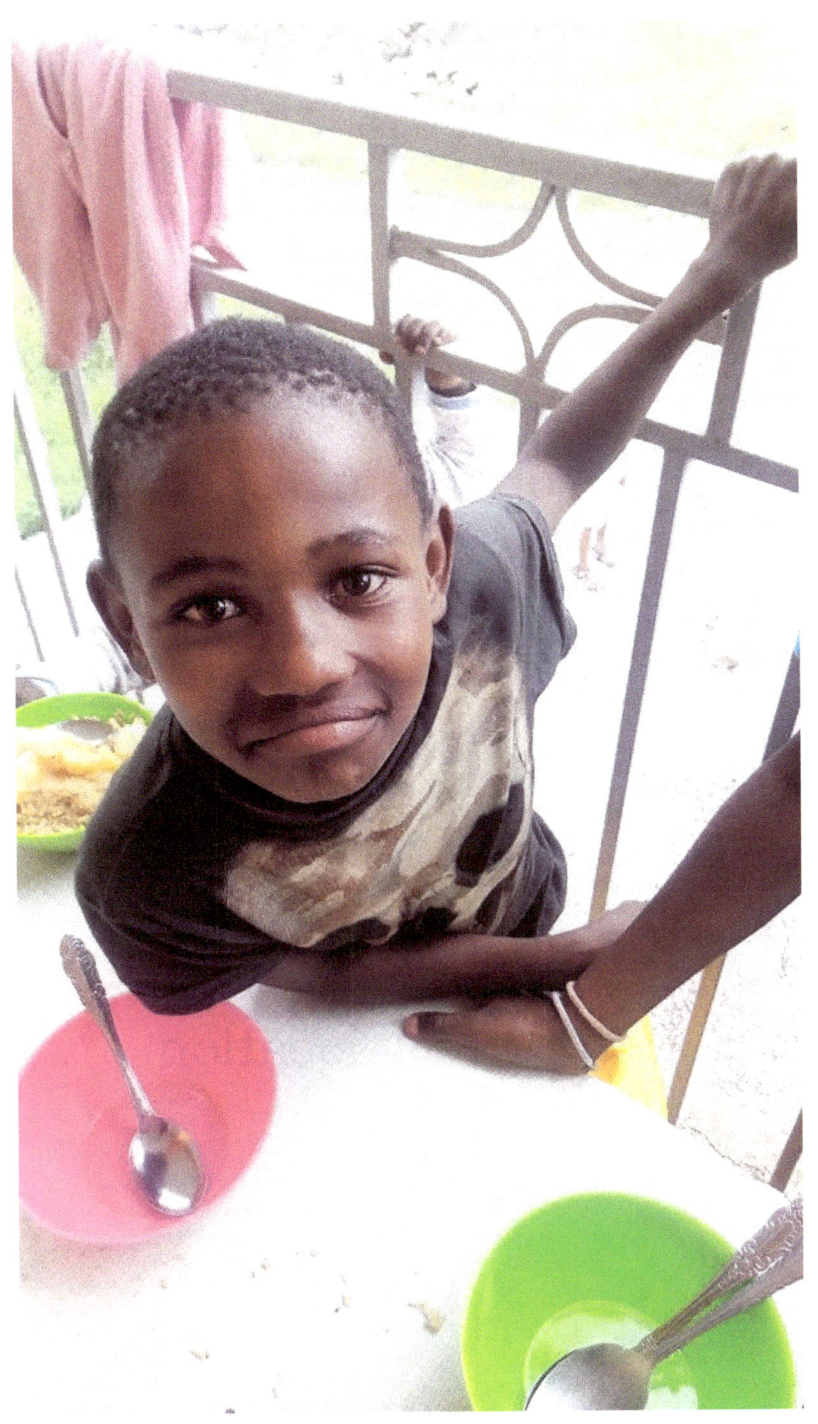

We find anywhere we can to eat our dinners.

With so many of us around, space can be limited.

It is much better since we moved to our new location.

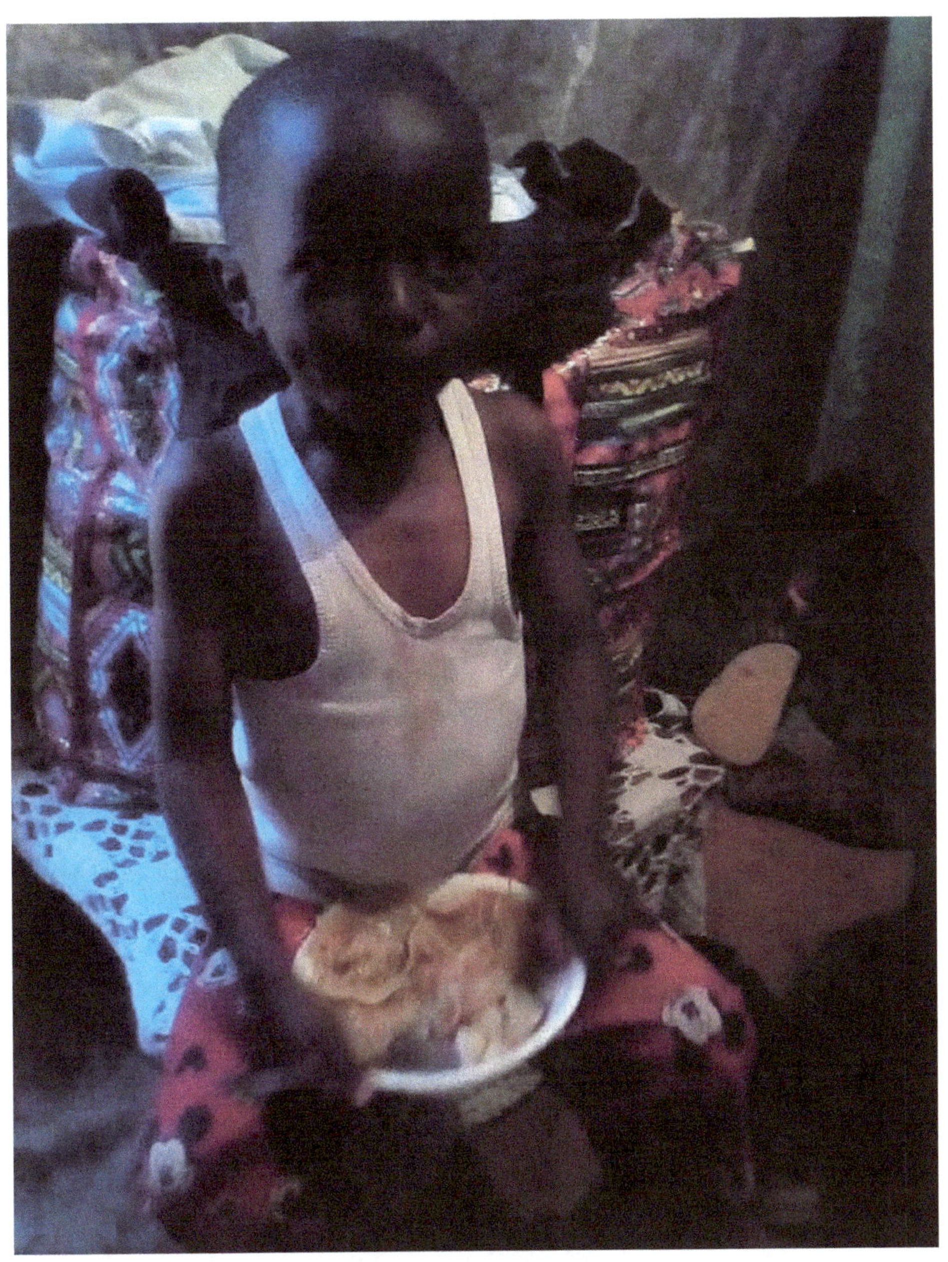

Dear Friends 22/01/1

Hello, My name is Nectarios Kitimo a years-old-boy at St. Tabitha ophanage church and School in Baby class.

I respect the people around me and wishing to go far in my education and become a doctor. Requesting you for more support. Thank you.

Yours sincerely,

Nectarios Kitimo.

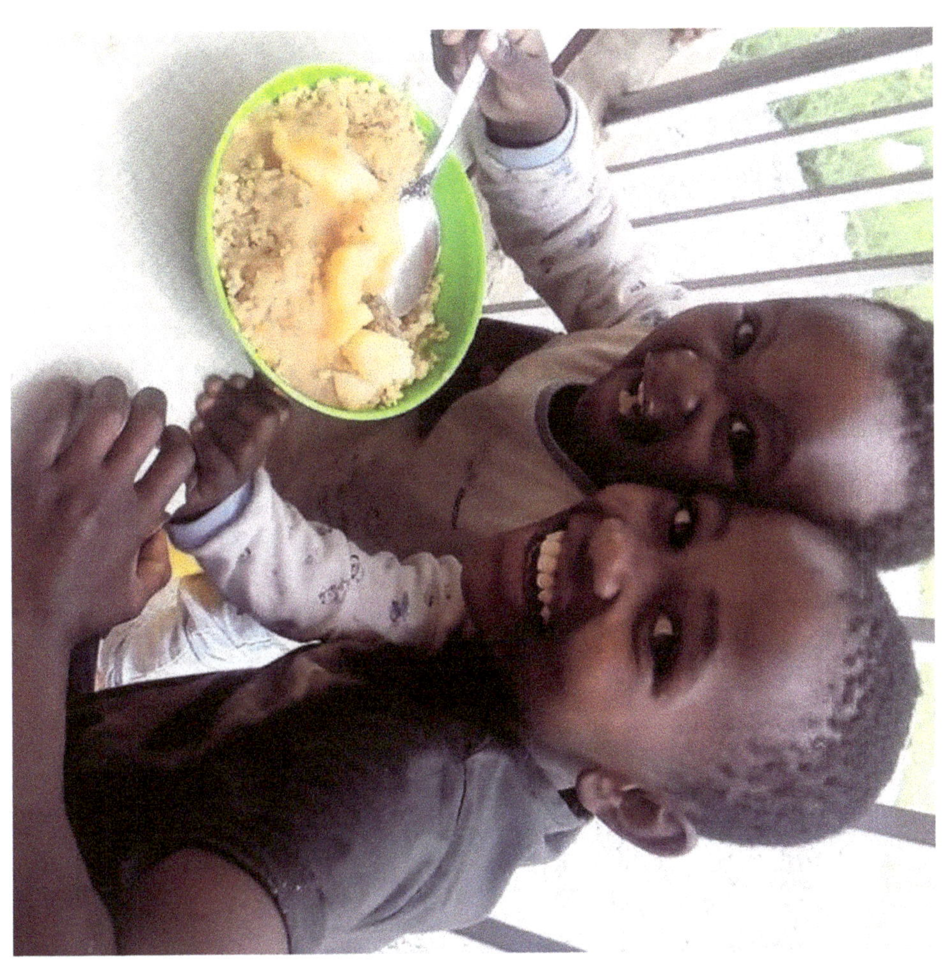

Eating breakfast is important.

It helps us to grow up strong so we will be tall.

If we eat fast, maybe we can have some more before all the morning's food is gone for today.

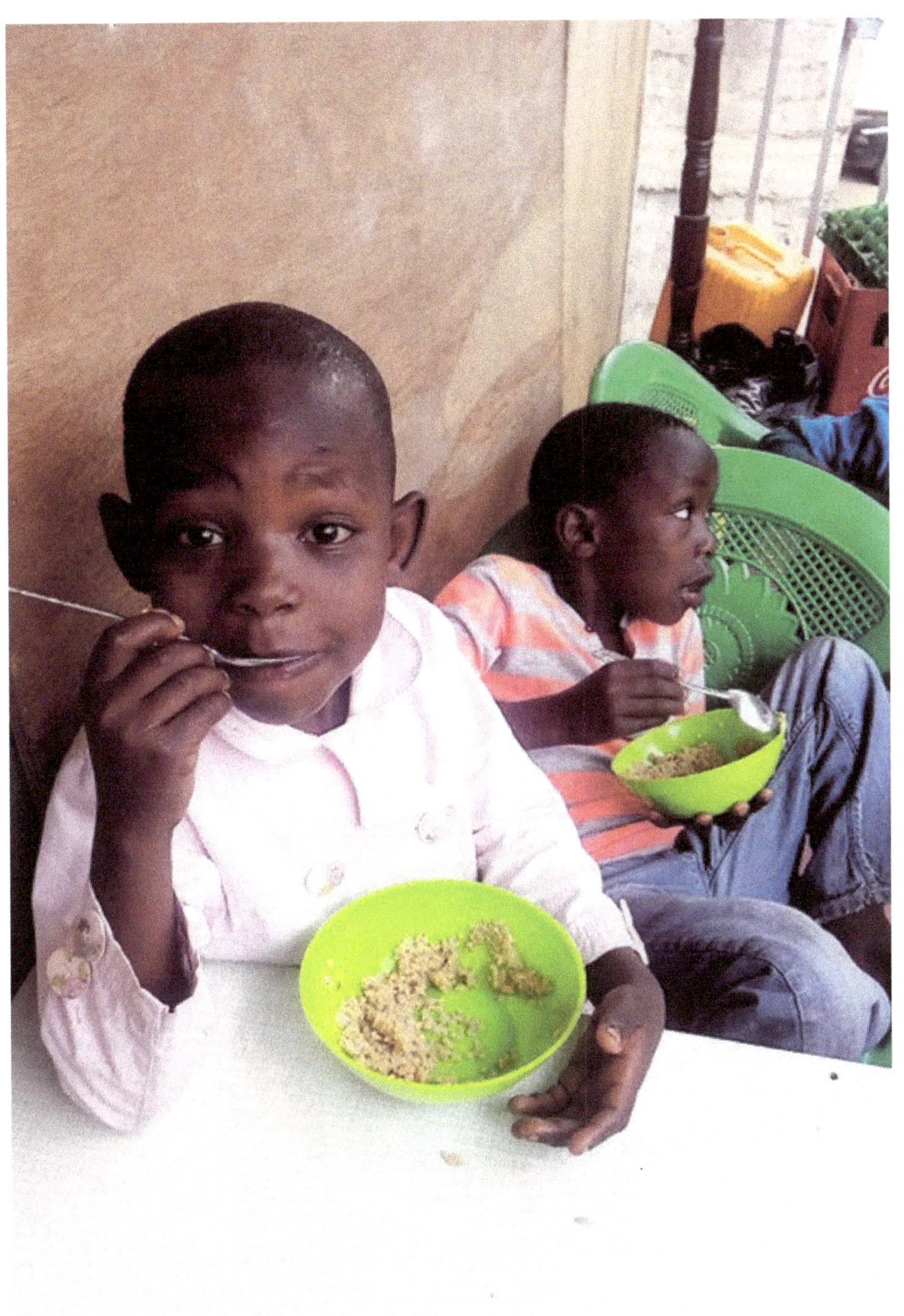

Dear friends -

22/06/2018.

· Hello, My name is Antiah · Branice. 9 years old. at St tabitha · othordox ophanage church and school. in class - 4 -

I respect people around me · and wishing to go far in my education · and become a ccountant · Requesting you for more support -

Thankyou ·

Yours sincerely ·

Antiah Branice ·

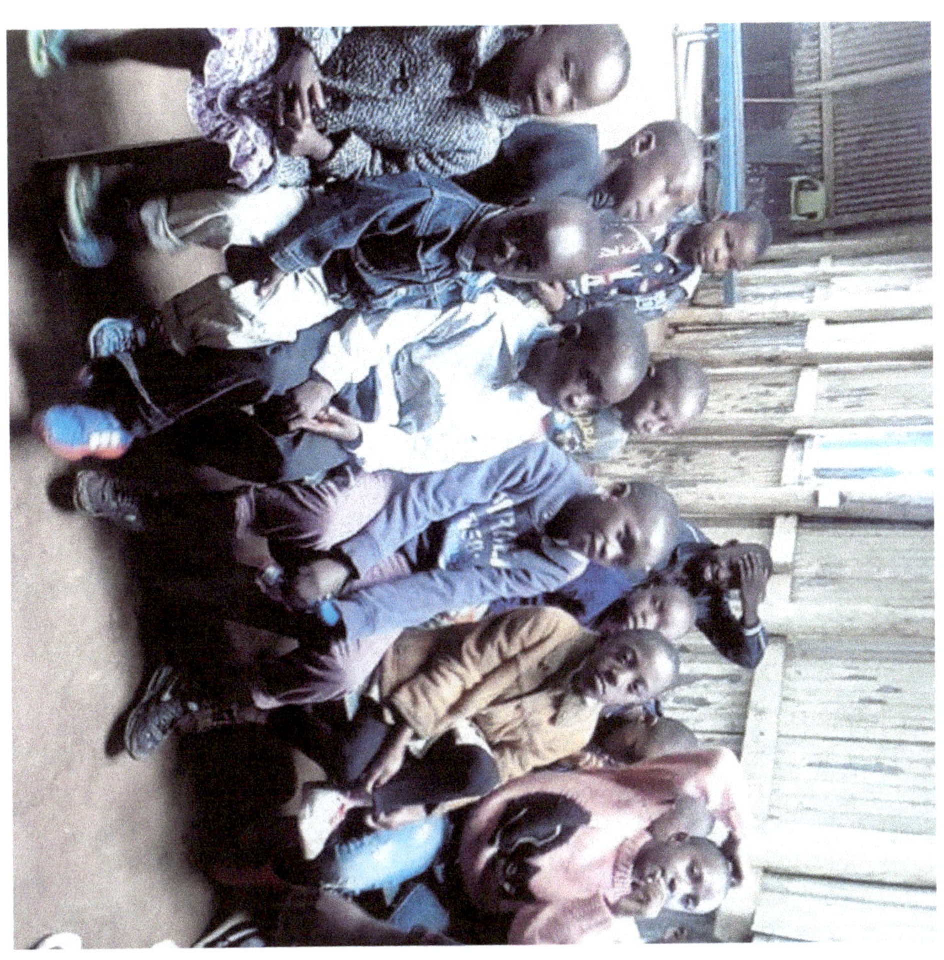

Little children always find a way to get dirty, especially when mud is the only thing around to play with.

Saint Tabitha's House provides all the children with soap and makes sure they wash regularly.

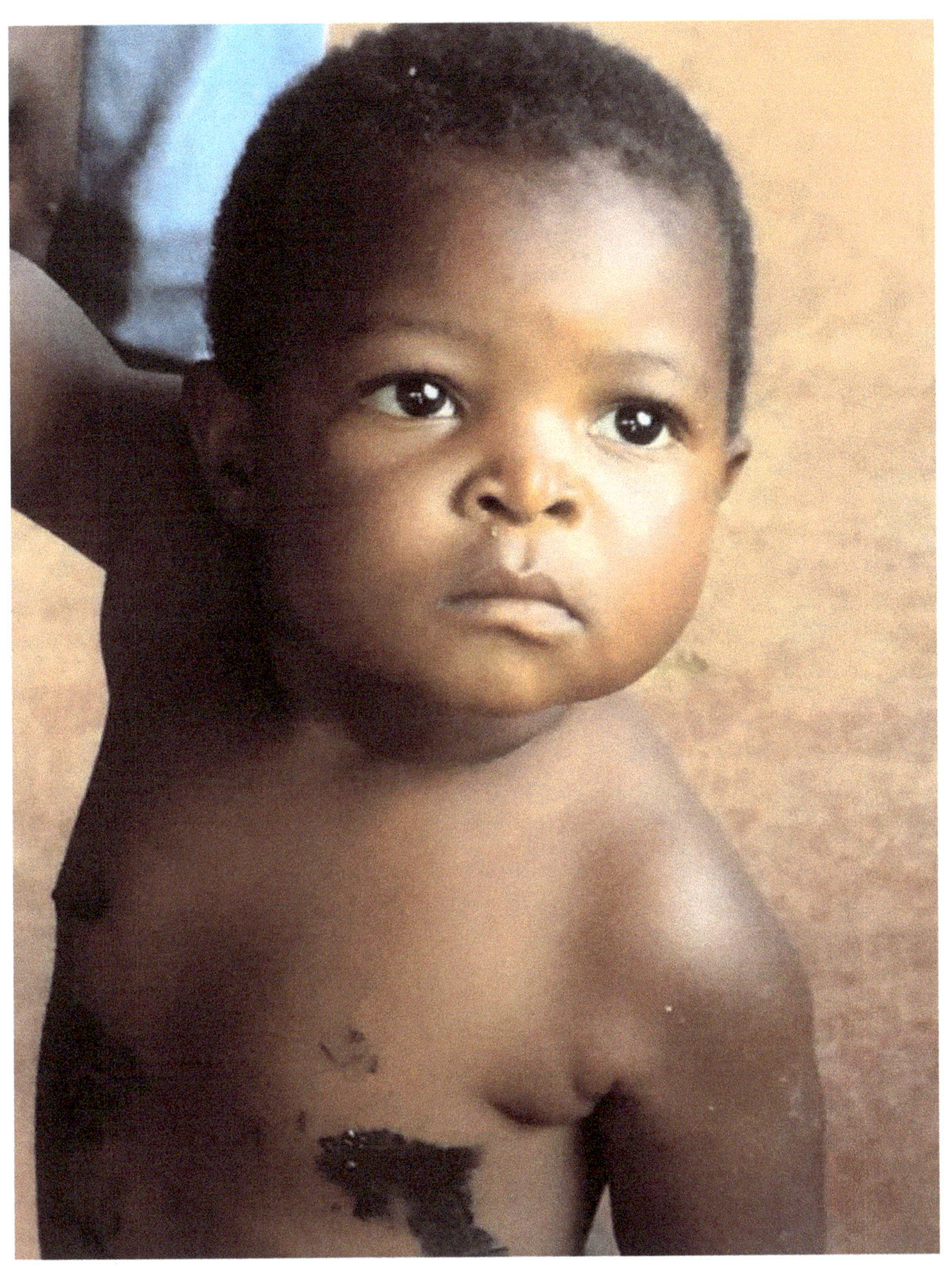

Dear friends, 25/4/2018.

Hi, My Name is Grace Awinja a fifteen years old girl at St-Tabitha Orthodox orphanage Church and School in Shirali secondary school in form I.

Last term in my exams I scored the following grades

1. mathematics D+
2. Kiswahili D+
3. English. C
4. Chemestry B
5. History C
6. Christian religious Education (C)
7. Biology D+
8. Physics. D+
9. Agriculture C
10. Geography C
11. Computer studies D

The mean grade was (C) but I will put more effort to score high grades. and be a successful person in future.

I respect the people around me and wishing to go far. Not forgetting I Like Playing football ~~that~~ Keeps my Leisure time. ~~Req~~ Requesting you for more support. Thank you.

Yours Sincerely,
Grace Awinja.

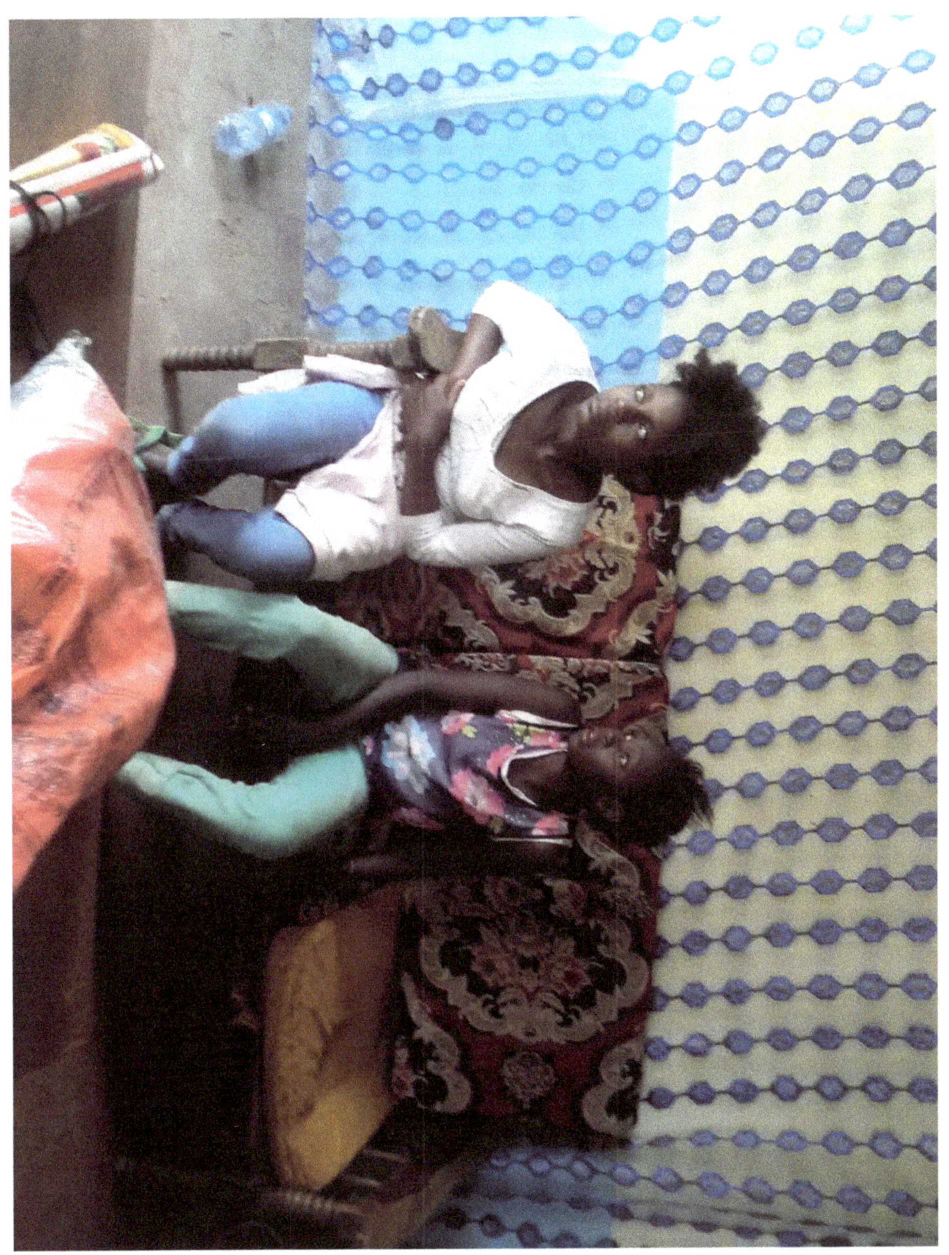

We sing Christmas carols together
at the end of every year.

Some of us wear red hats when we sing
for other people.

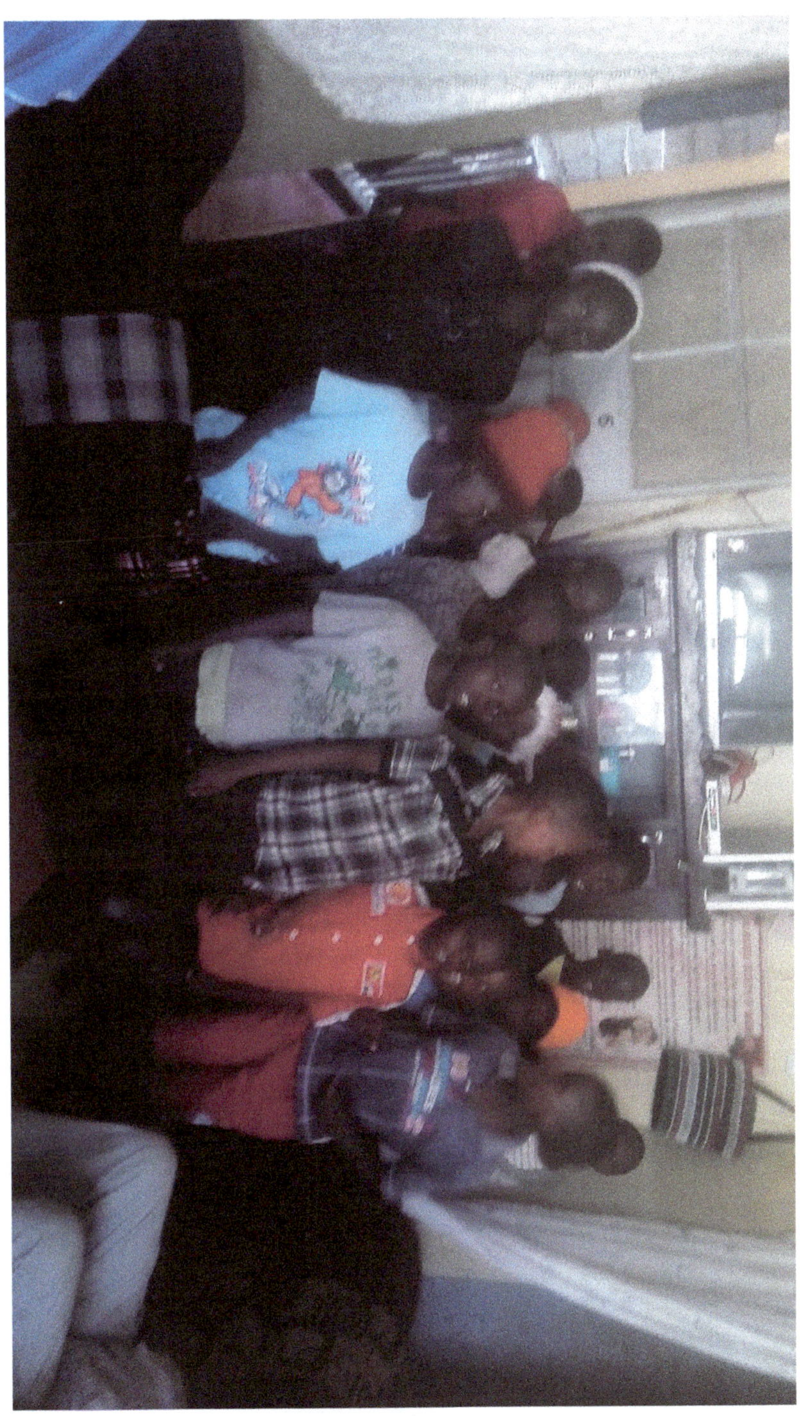

Even our youngest sisters enjoy drinking the milk provided by the cow at our new home.

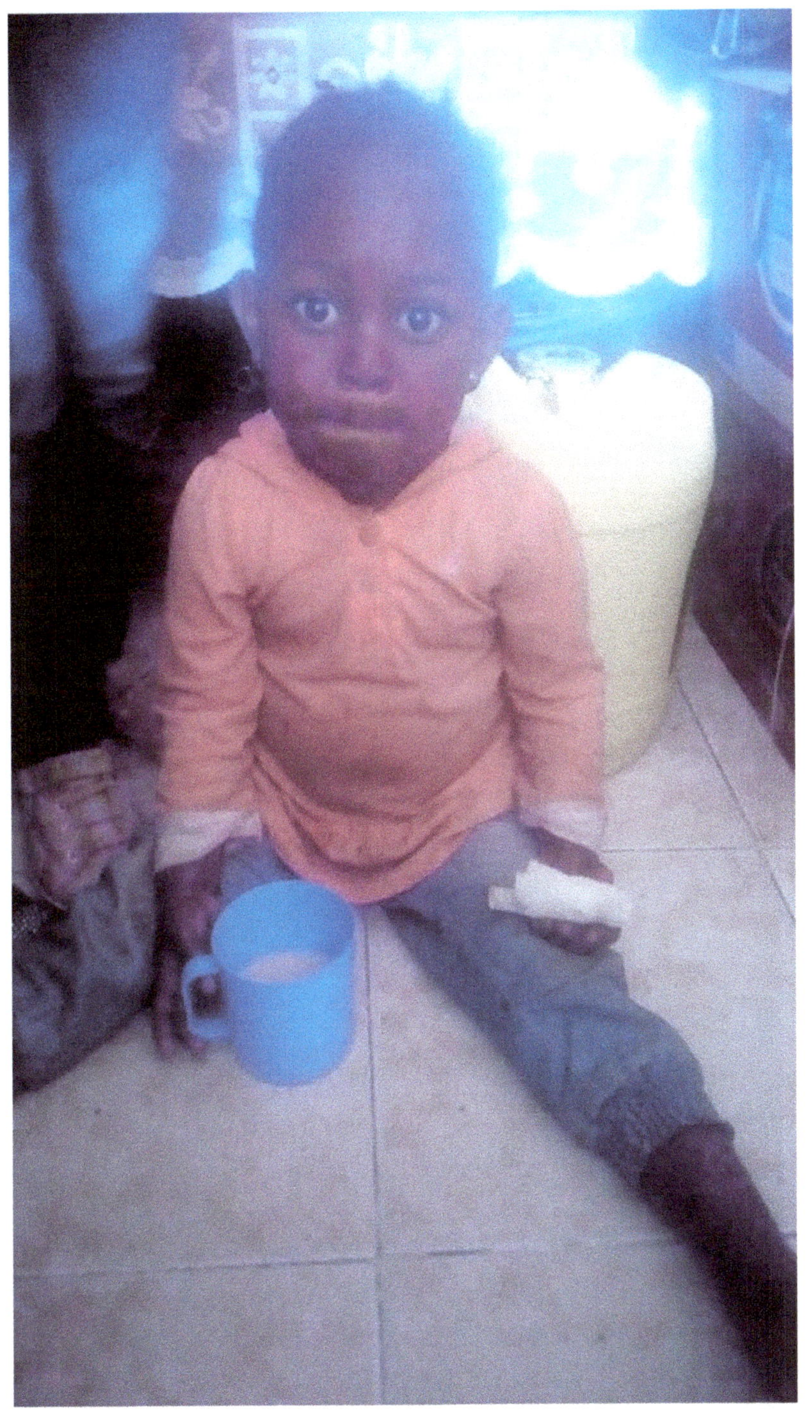

22/6/2018

Dear Friends

Hello my name is CHRISTOTHEA Namagi a six years old girl at ST. Tabitha orthodox orphanage church and school in class one. I respect the people around me and become a pilot. Request you for more support thank you.

yours sincerely

CHRISTOTHEA Namagi

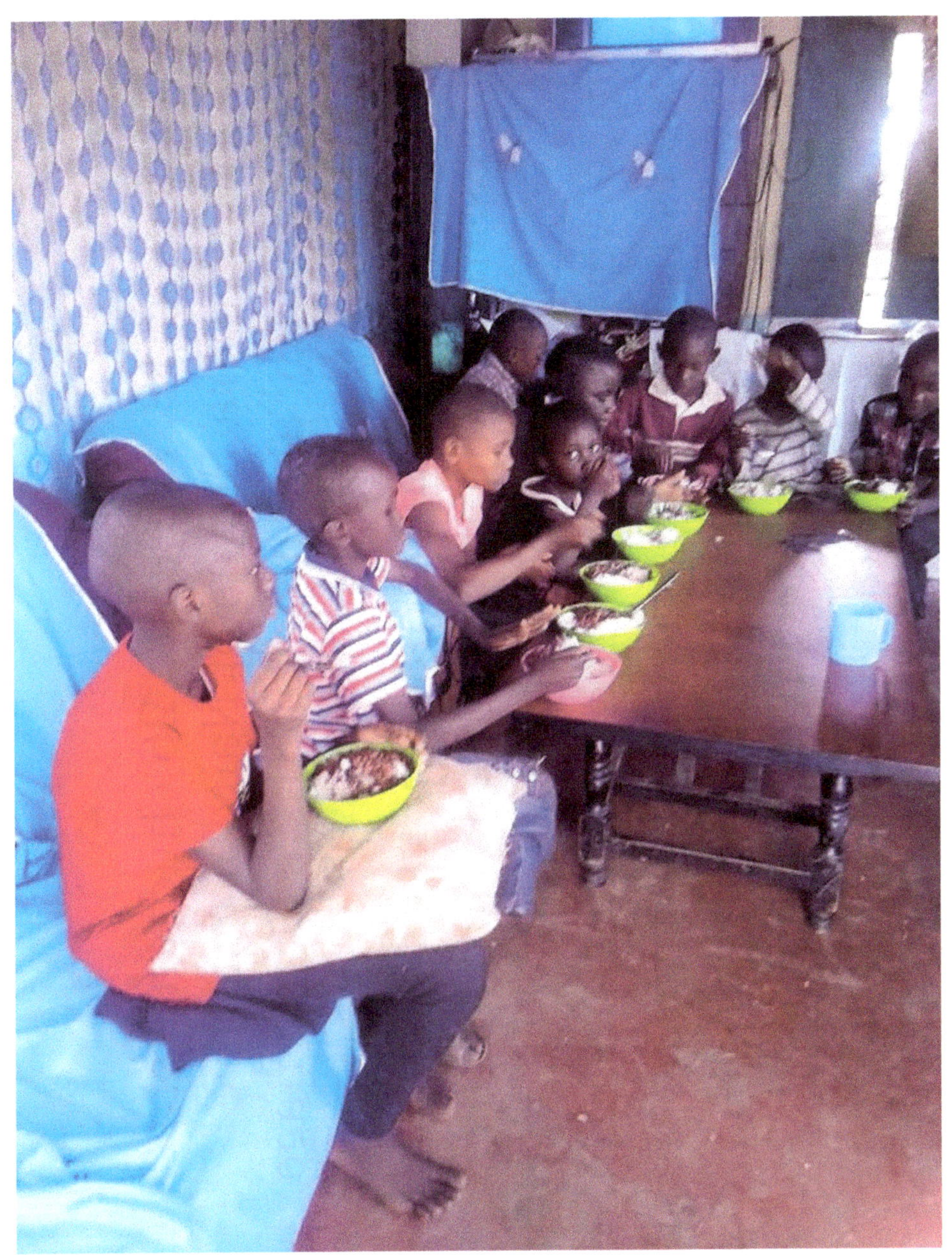

As of 2018, there are 26 children from the Kibera Slums of Nairobi who live permanently at Saint Tabitha's Orphanage.

Some children have received the blessing of adoption into a loving family.

We are always a little sad when one of our brothers or sisters has to leave but we know that he or she will make another family very happy and have a wonderful life.

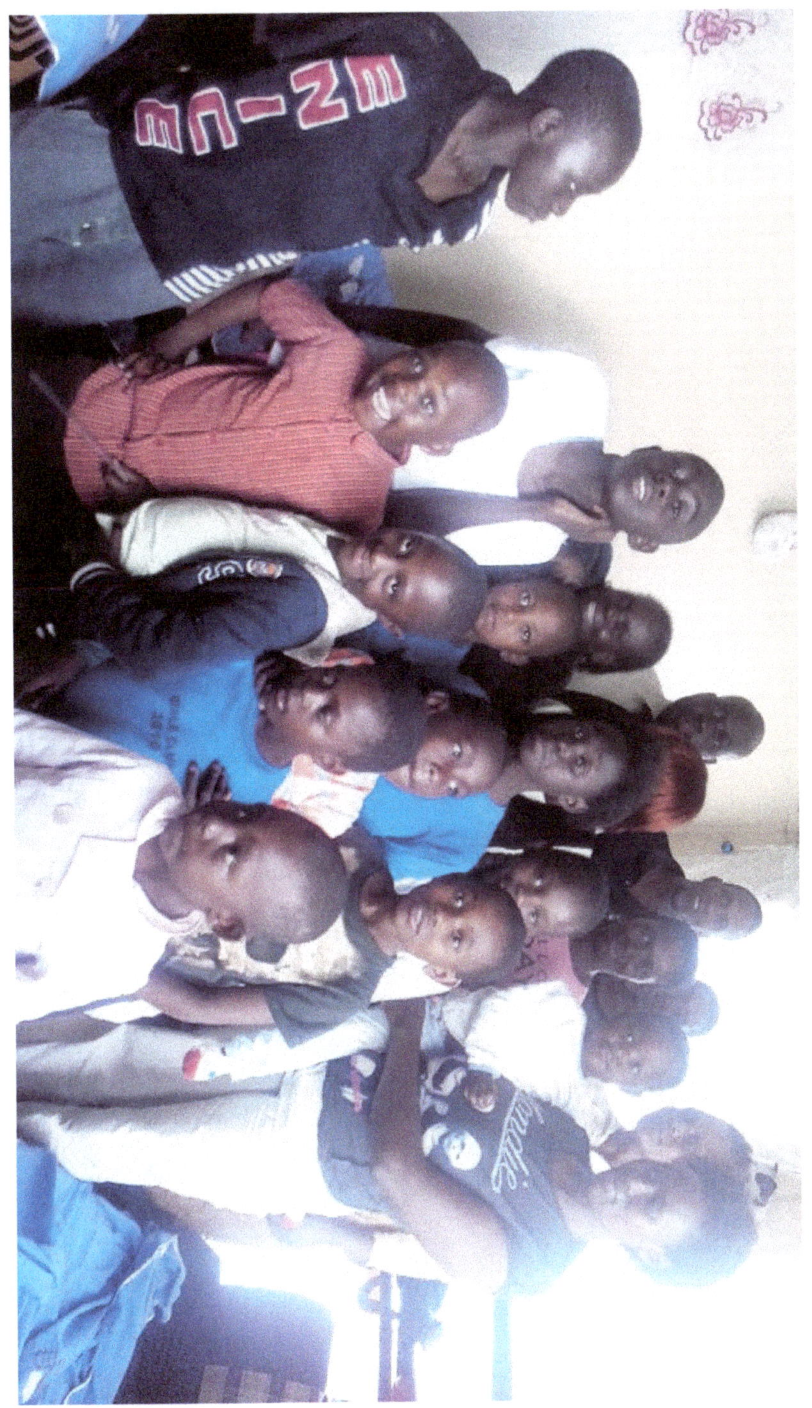

25/04/2018

Dear; Friends;

Hello, My name is Mishell Kwamboka. a 11 years Old-girl at St. Tabitha orthodox orphanage church and school in class 5.

I respect the people around me and wishing to go far in my education and become a teacher. Requesting you for more support. Thank you.

Yours Sincerely.
Mishell Kwamboka.

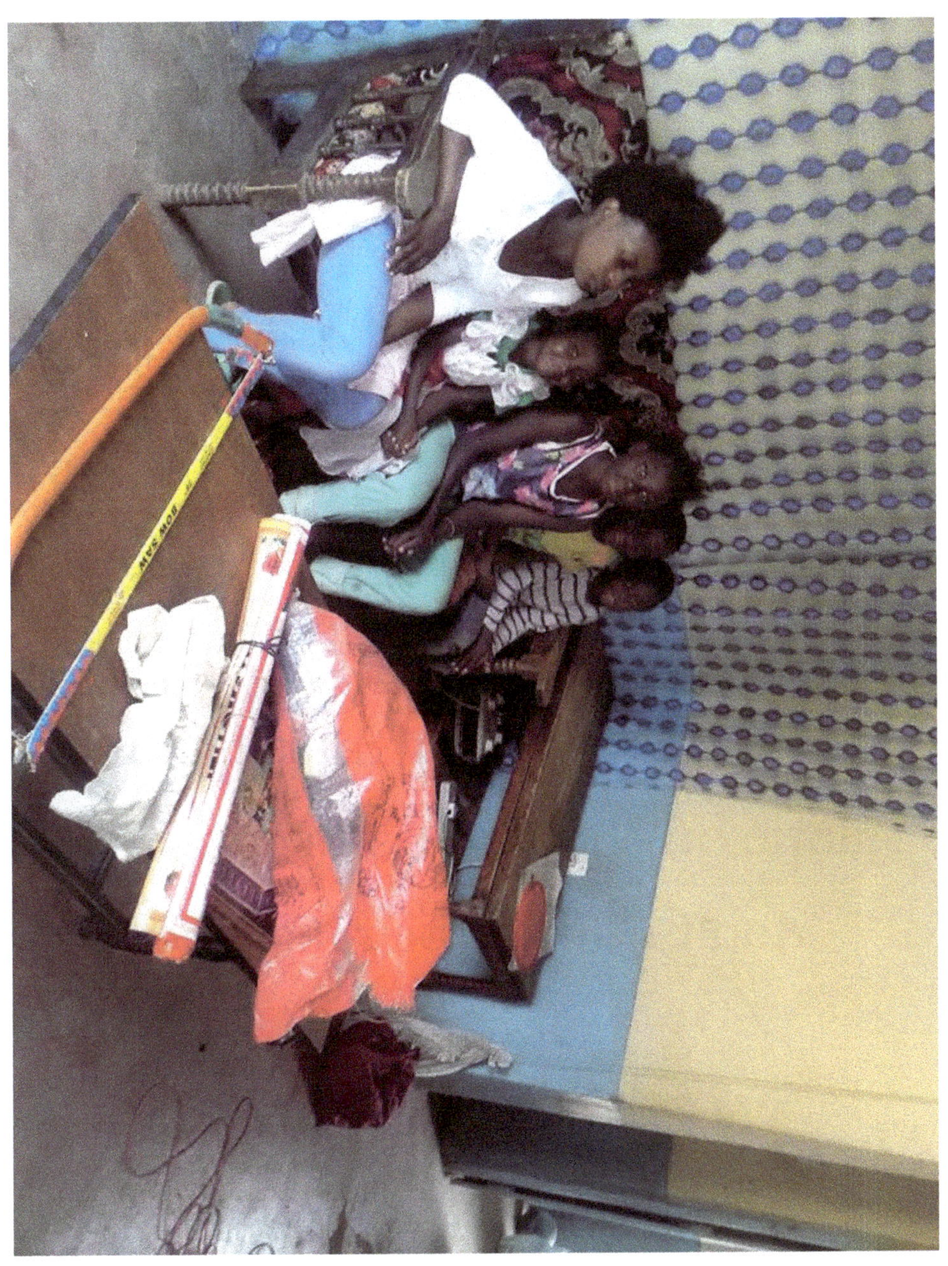

It is good to be able to make friends with all the other children at Saint Tabitha's Orphanage.

It is much better than life all alone on the streets because we don't have to beg for food.

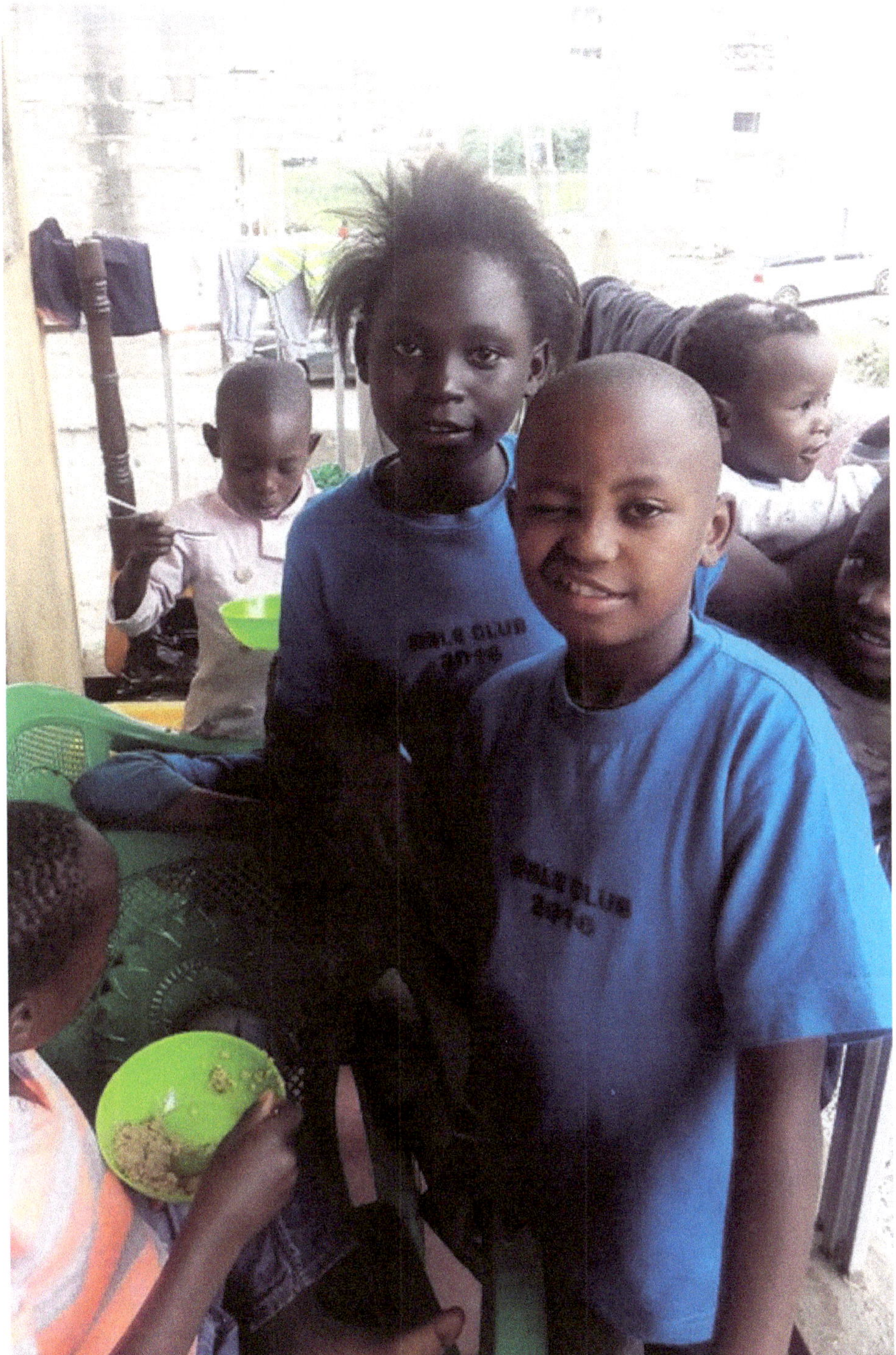

Dear Friends 22/6/2012

Hello, My name is Proxedes a 5 years -old-girl of St. Tabitha Orphanage church and School in Baby class.

I respect the people around me and wishing to go for in my education and become a pilot. Requesting you for more support. Thank you.

Your sincerely,

Proxedes

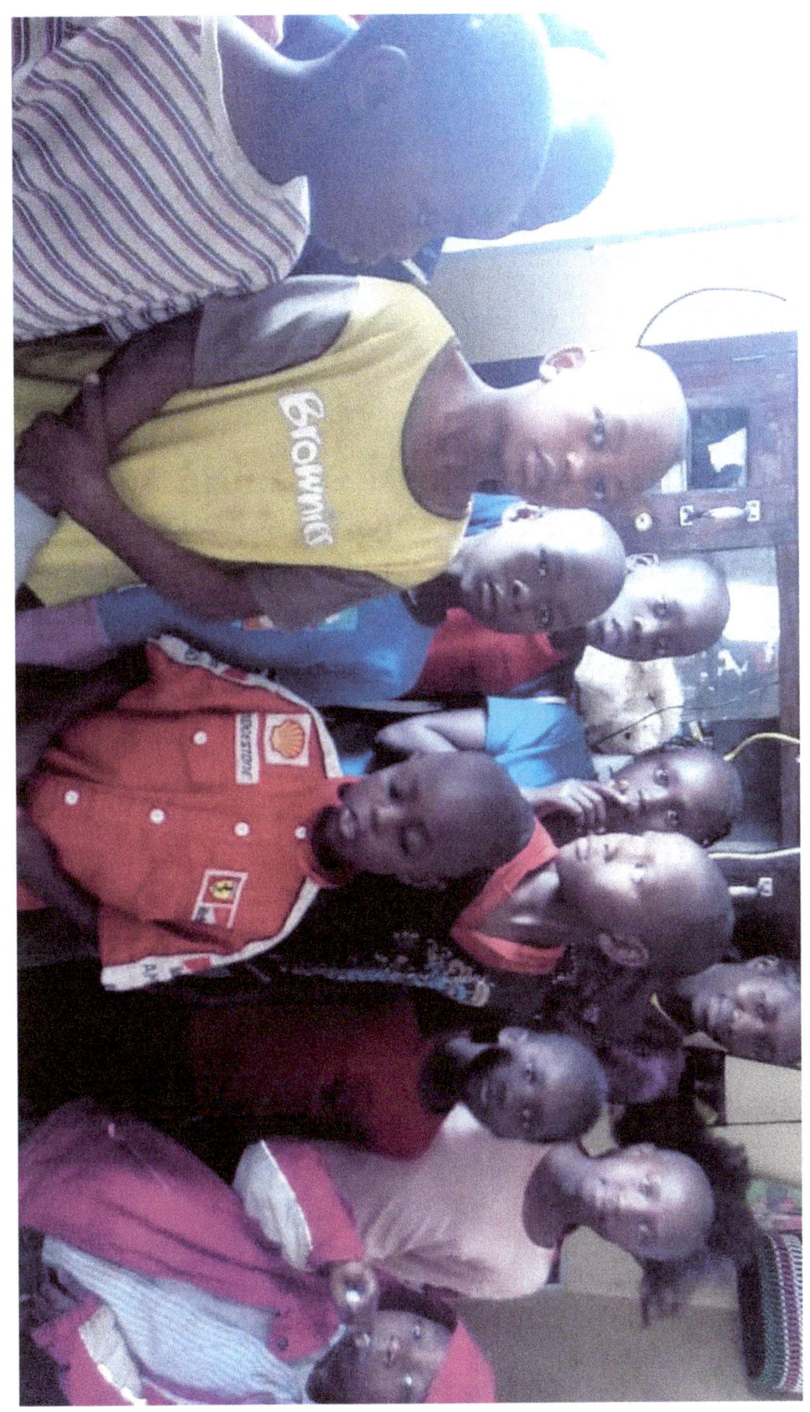
Browning

Sometimes, the Lord blesses us with warm sunshine and sweet juicy fruits.

We hope that some day we may always be able to eat so well.

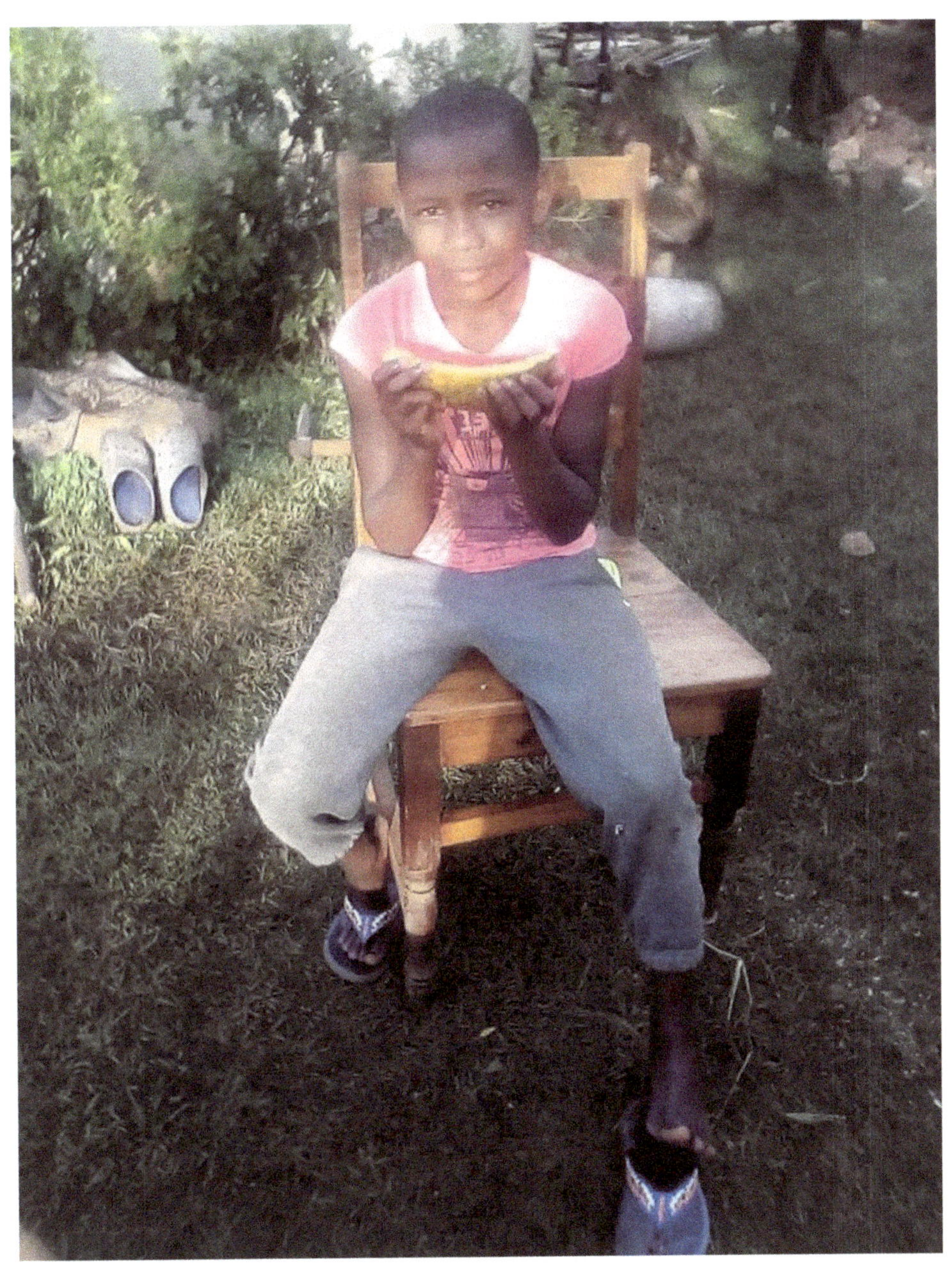

Our Education

Our school uniforms make us feel like we all belong
together so we take care of them well.
Every year we get a new uniforms to grow into.
Each uniform costs $15.
But school fees cost much more.
They are $150 per year for every
child in primary school and
$400 per year for every high school student.

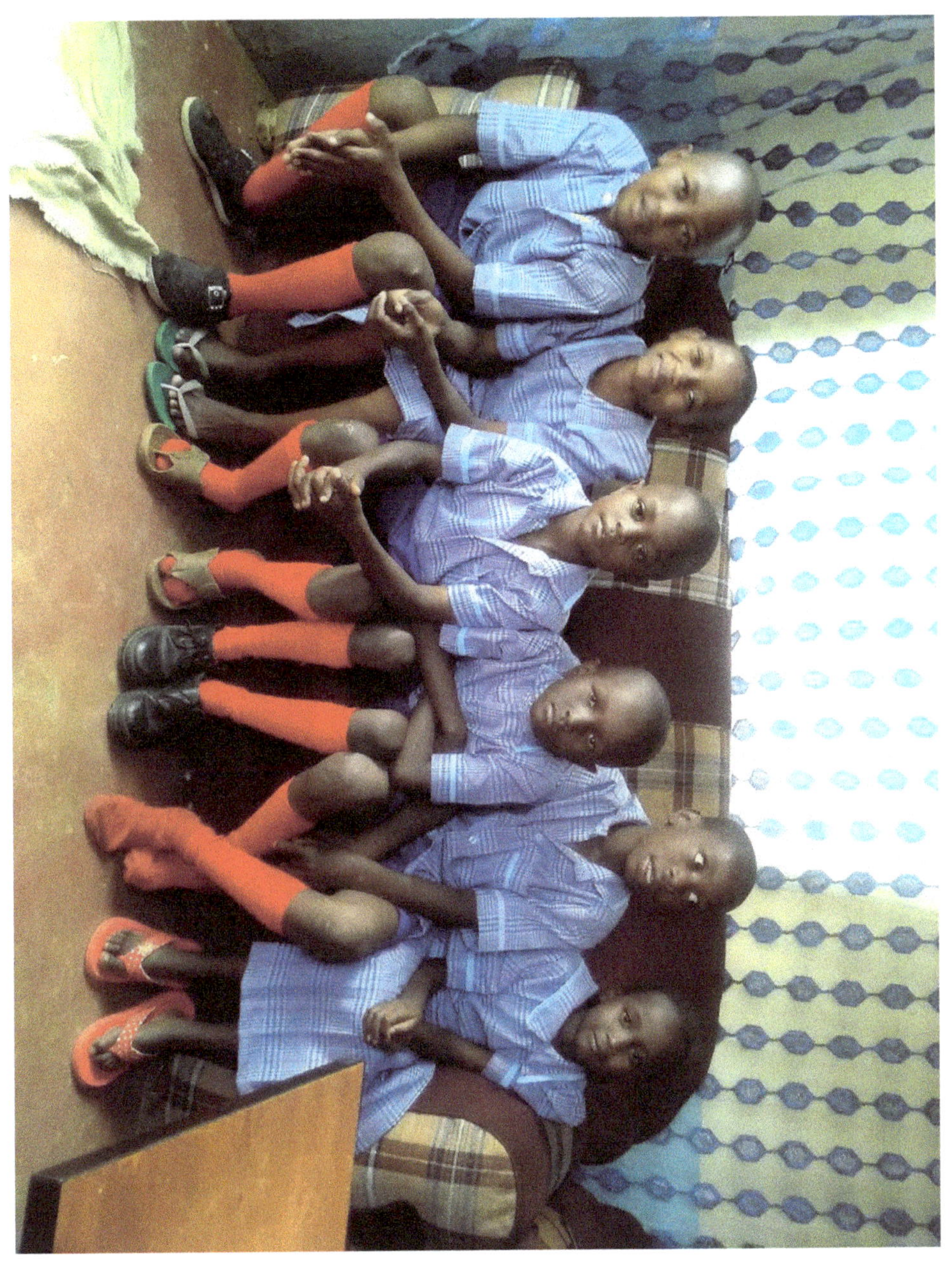

25/4/2010

Dear friends,

Hello, my name is Ruth muchisu a 6 years old girl at St. Tabitha orthodox orphange church and school. in class one.

I respect the people around me. and wishing to become nurse. Requesting you for more support.

thank you.

Your's sincerely

Ruth muchisu

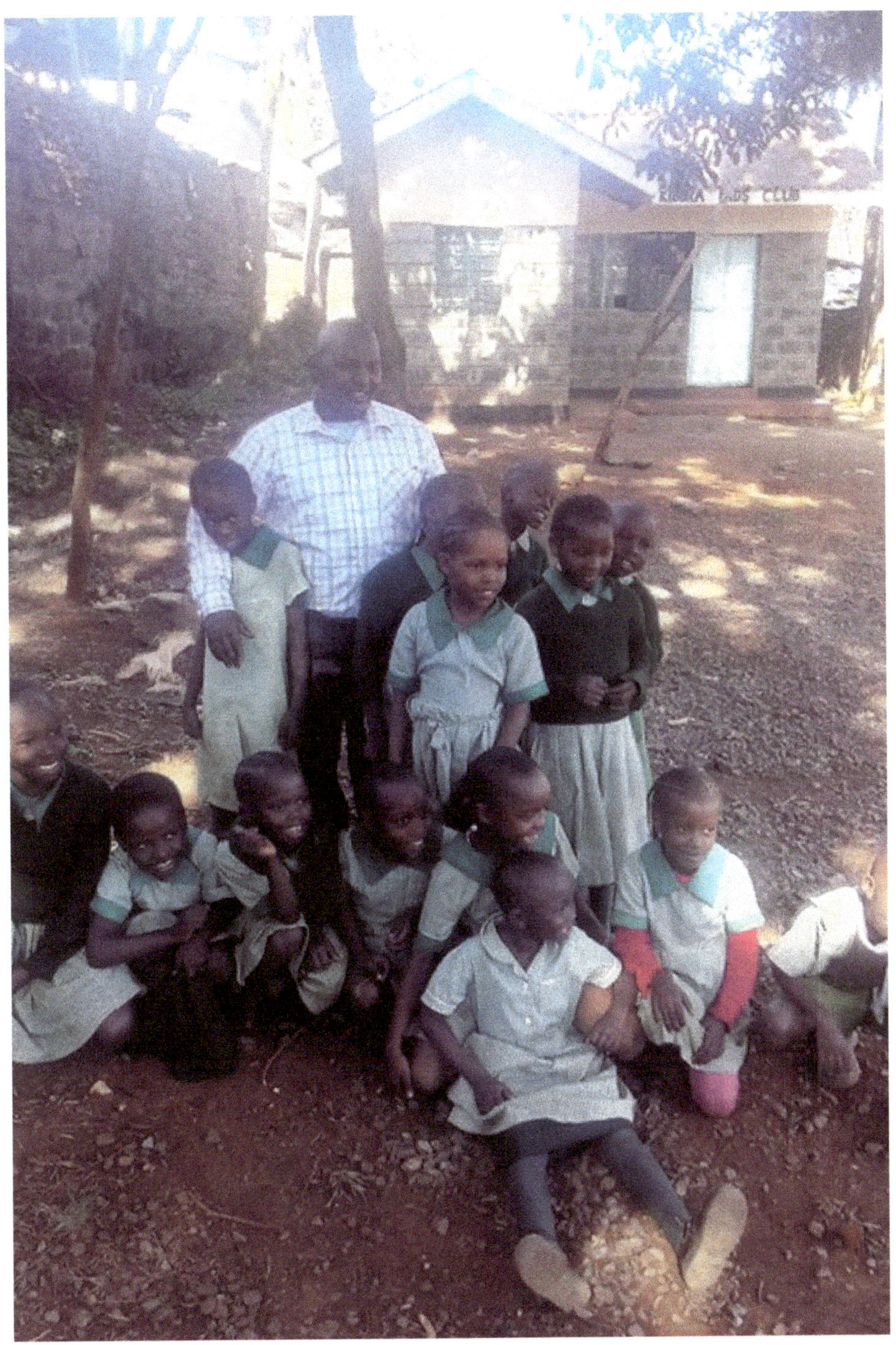

25th/4/2018.

Dear friends,

Hi, my name is Jenipher Aloo a ninenteen years old girl at St. Tabitha Orthodox Orphanage Church and School in form one at Shirali Secondary School.

Last term I did exam and managed to Score the following grades in my Subjects:

1. Mathematics. A.
2. English. B+.
3. Kiswahili A.
4. Biology. A.
5. Chemistry. A.
6. Physics. A.
7. History A.
8. Geography. A.
9. Christian Religious education (C.R.E) A
10. Computer studies A-
11. Business Studies. A-

The mean grade was A- but I will put more effort in the rest of my studies and be a Successful person in future.

I respect the people around me and wishing to achieve my ambition of becoming a Surgion. Not forgetting my hobby, I like reading novels that keeps my leisure time. With those few remarks, requesting you for more Support. Thank you.

Yours Sincerely,
Jenipher Aloo.

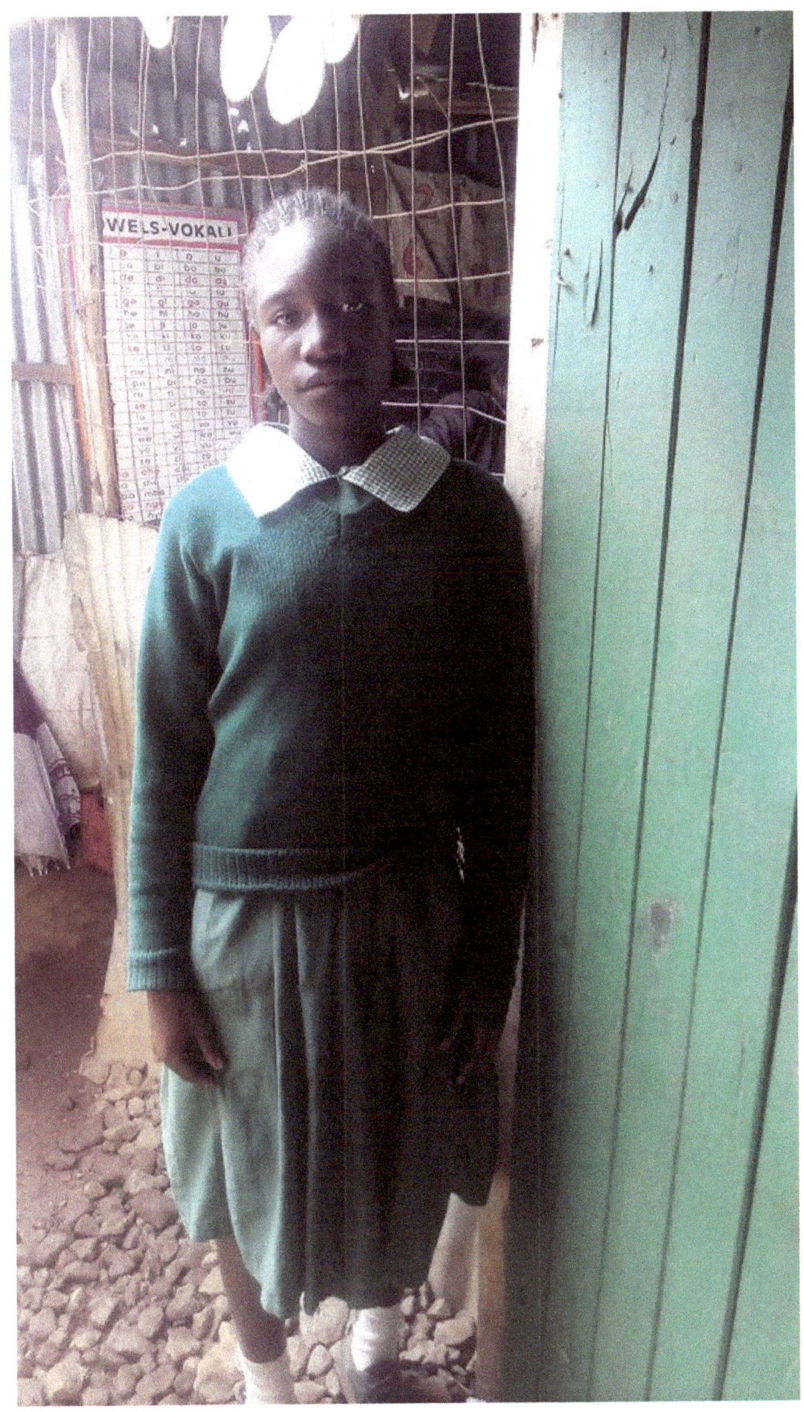
WELS-VOKALI

Fr Agapios wishes to send a special thanks to Barbara Pappas.

Barbara has donated many very good books to Saint Tabitha's Orphanage and School.

Without supplies like these it would be much harder to educate the children.

The children are all so very thankful for her kindness.

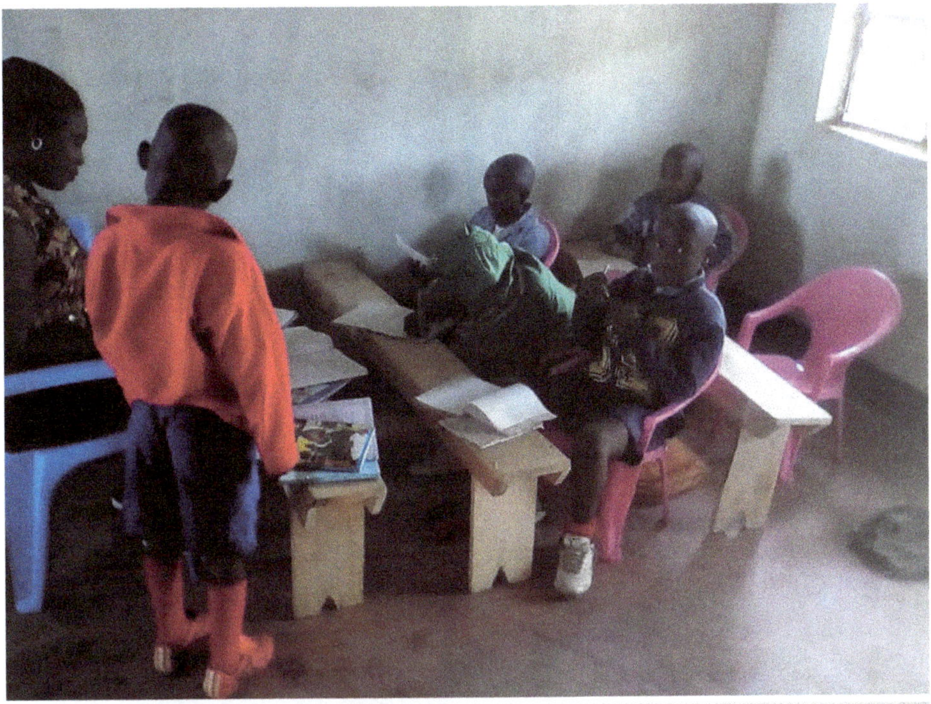

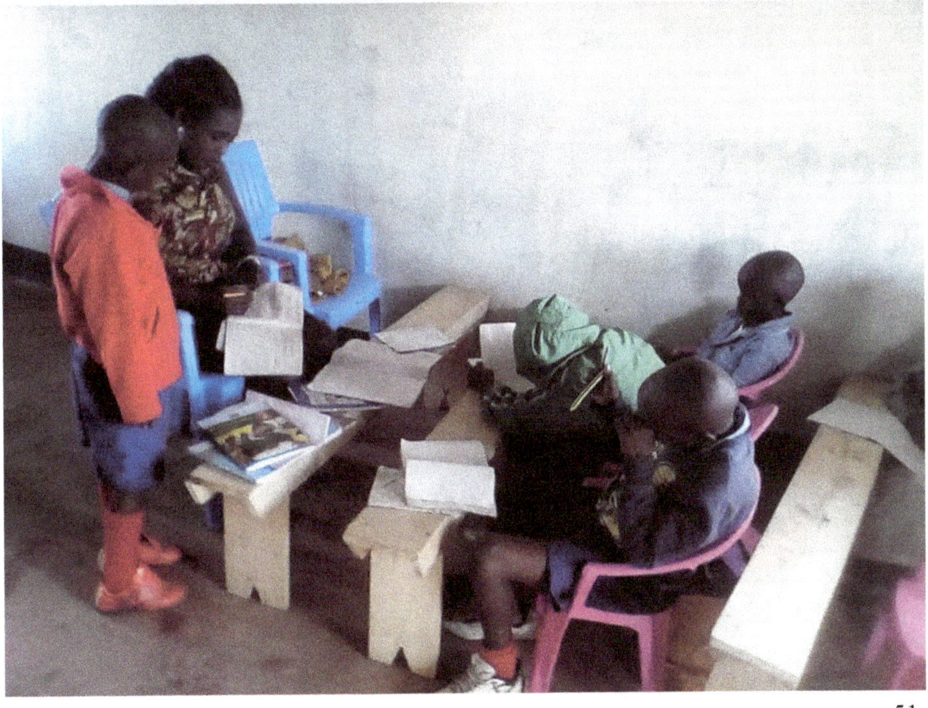

Dear friends- 22/ /2018.

·Hello, my name is Trevor Baraza·

a 5 years old at St Tabitha othordox

ophanage church and school- in Top class.

I respect the people around me· and wishin

to go far in my education, and beome a

president. Requesting you for more support!

Thank you

Yours Sincerely.

Trevor Baraza

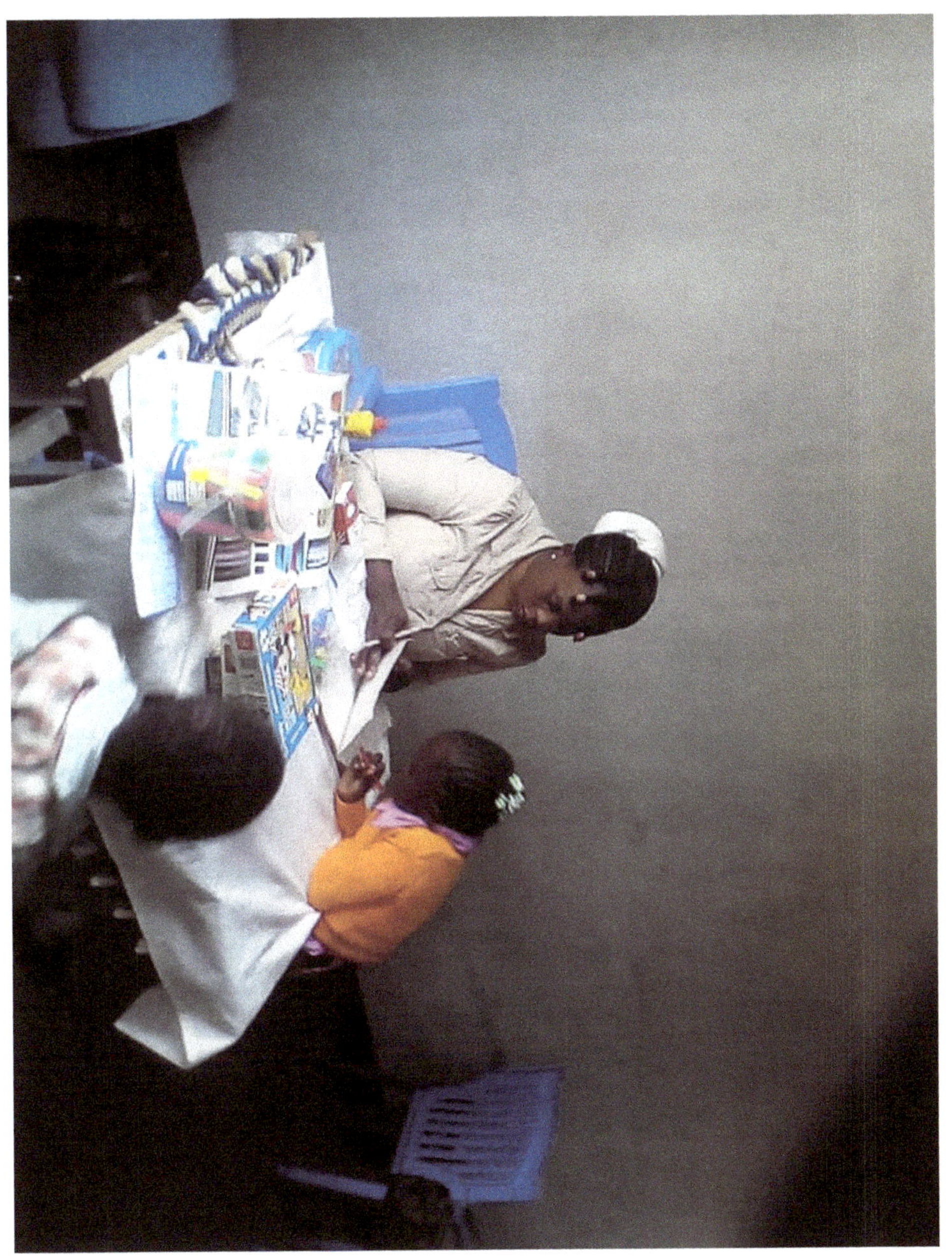

25/4/2018

Dear Friends,

Hello, My name is Theodoros ominde a 12 years-old-boy at s.t Tabitha Orthodox orphanage church and school in class 5.

I respect the people around me and wishing to go far in my education and become a doctor. Requesting you for more support. Thank you

Yours Sincerely.
Theodoros ominde

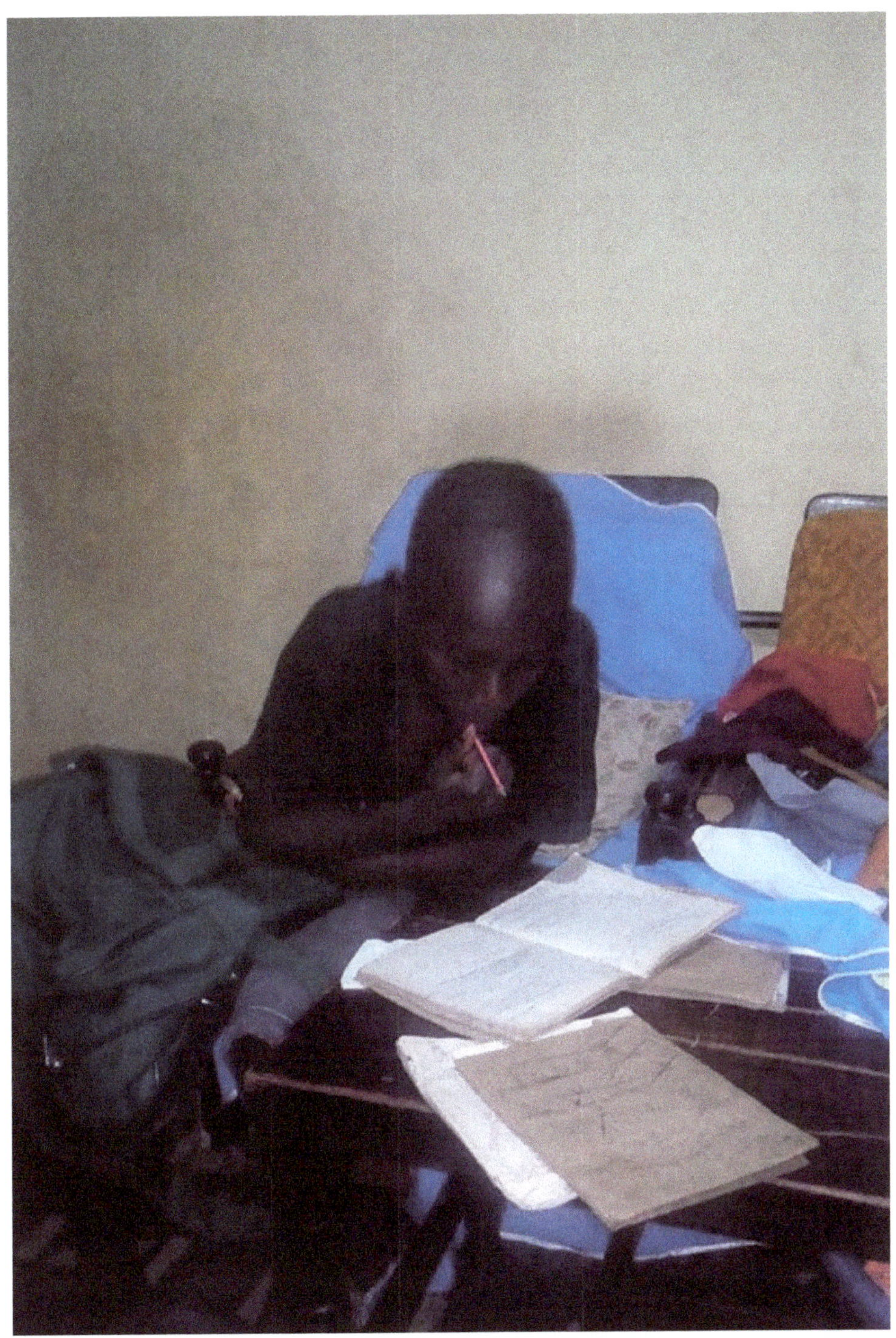

Our Community

22/6/2018

Dear friend

Hello my name is Agineta a 8 years girl at St Tabitha orthodox orPhanage church and School in class two. I respect the people arond me and become a teacher Requesting you for more support. thank

your Sincerelyx)

Agineta

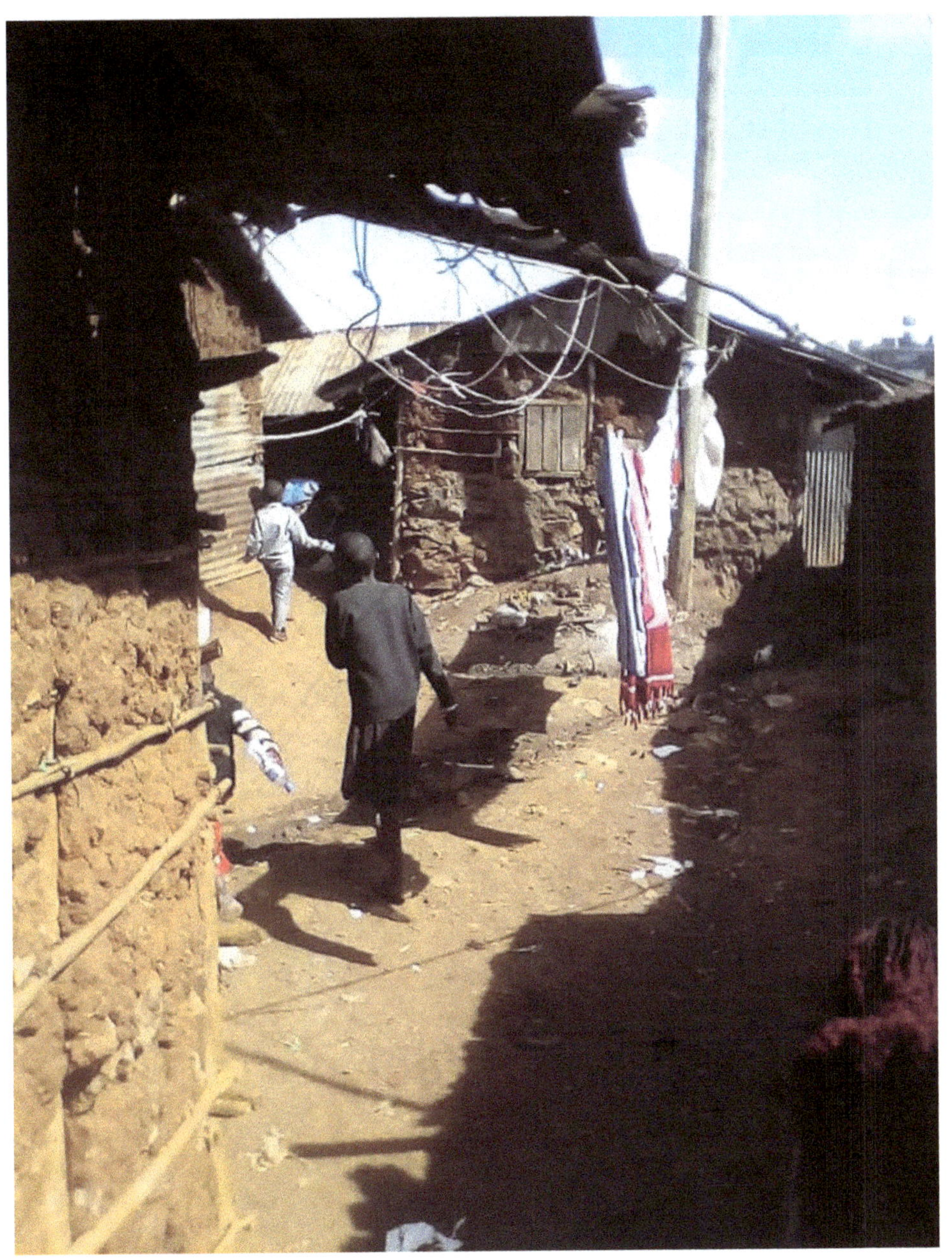

Father Agapios was assigned as the rector of Saint George the Great Martyr Parish in the Kibera Slums of Kenya.

That is where he started Saint Tabitha's Orphanage.

Since then, he has also travelled to serve the Lord Jesus Christ in many other parts of the country.

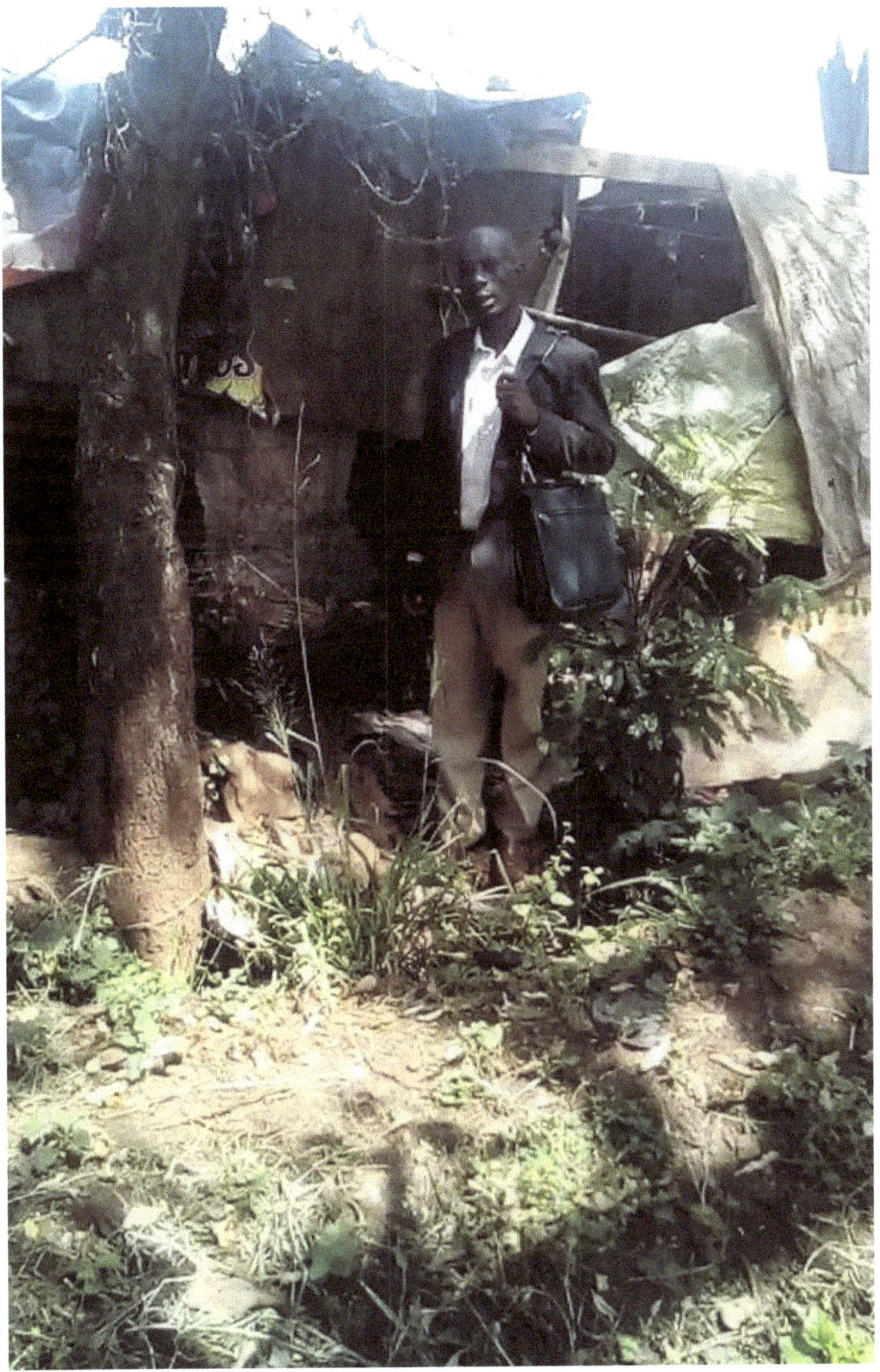

The Lord has blessed Fr Agapios with a wife and family who love and serve Jesus Christ too.

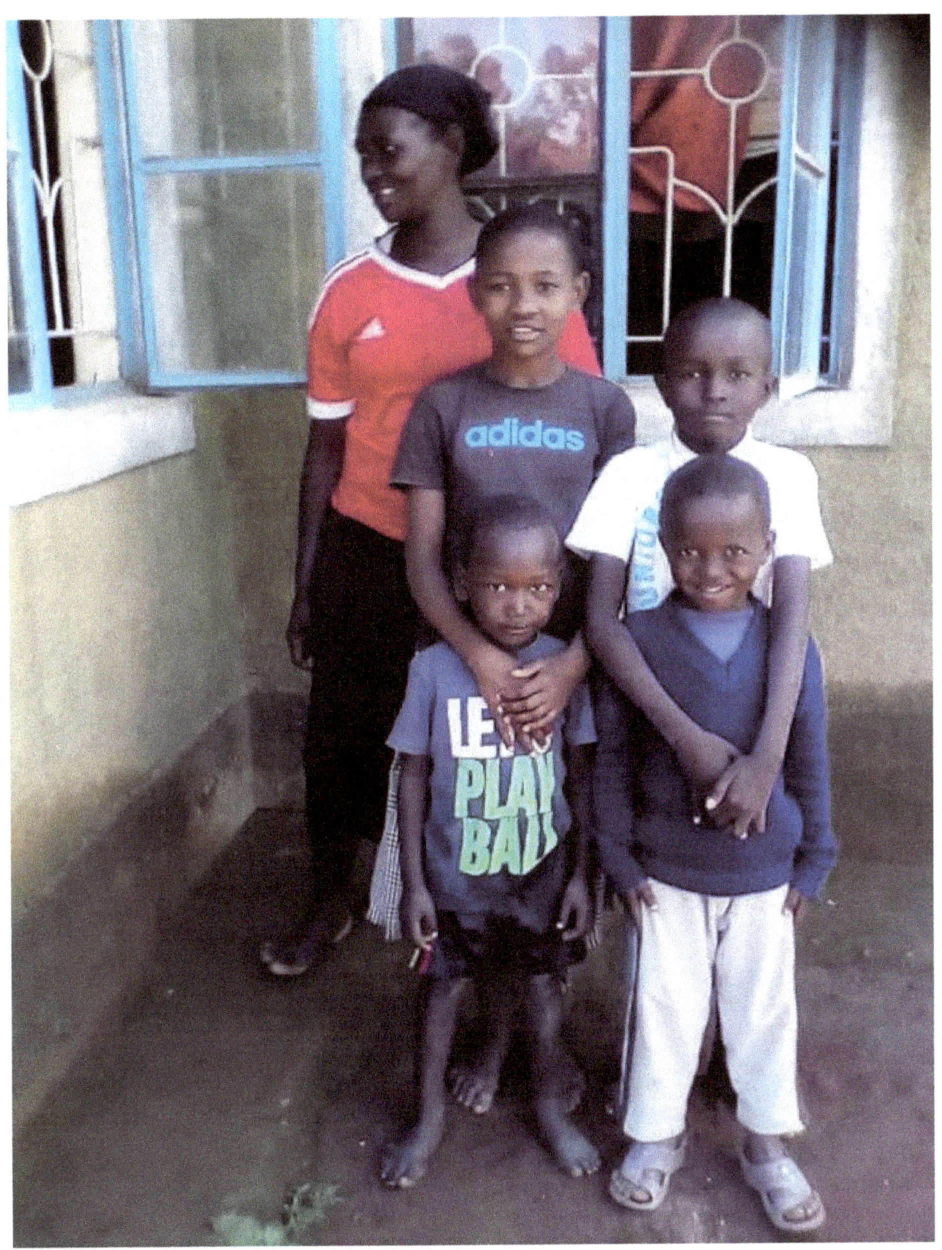
adidas
PLAY

25/4/2018

Dear, friends,

Hello, my name is Grace Ayuma a 9 years - old - girl at S.T. Tabitha orthodox orphanage church and school in class 3. I respect the people around me and wishing to go far in my education and become a pilot. Requesting you for more support. Thank you

Yours sincerely
Grace Ayuma

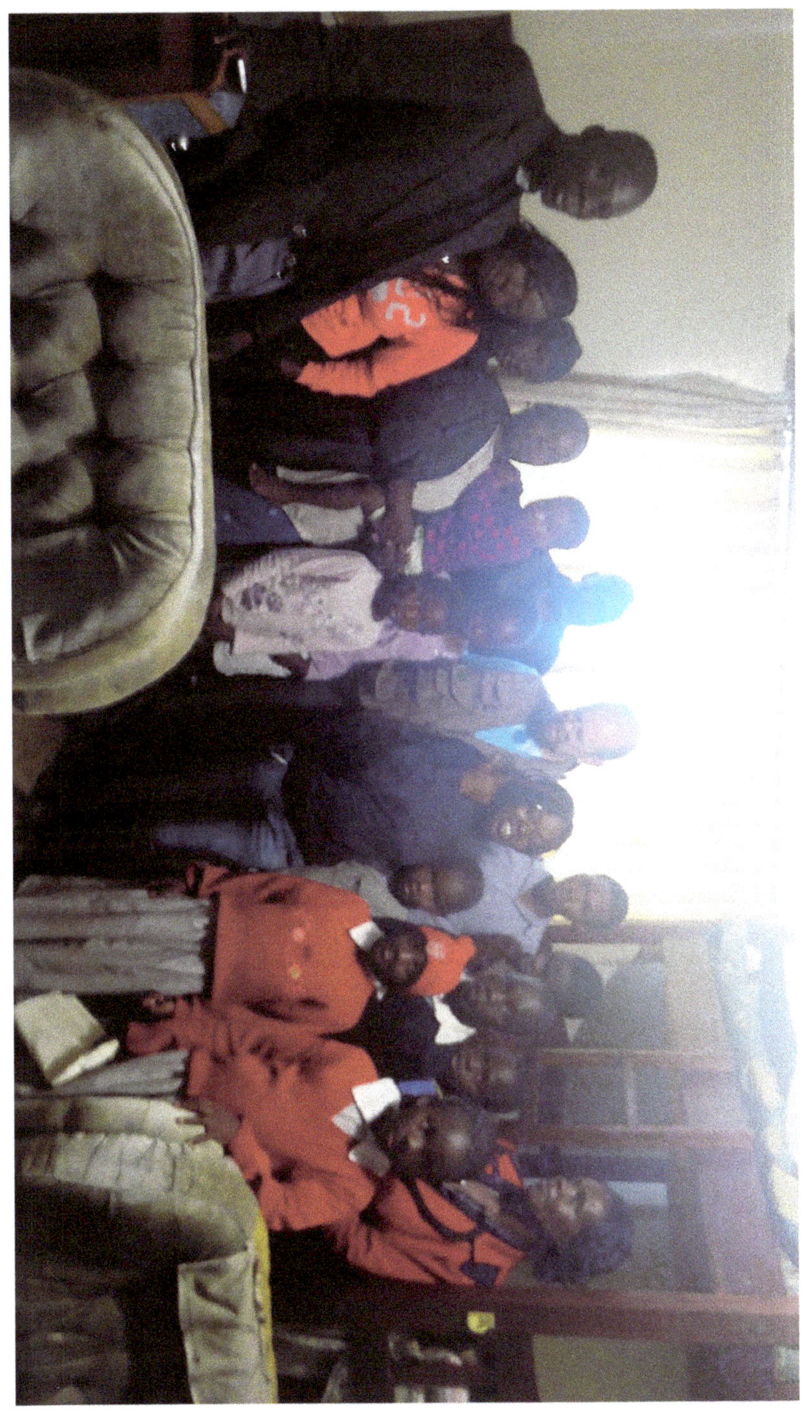

Kind and generous people sometimes help us with things like washing clothes or finding other people to help support our orphanage.

We are thankful for all the people the Lord sends to bless us.

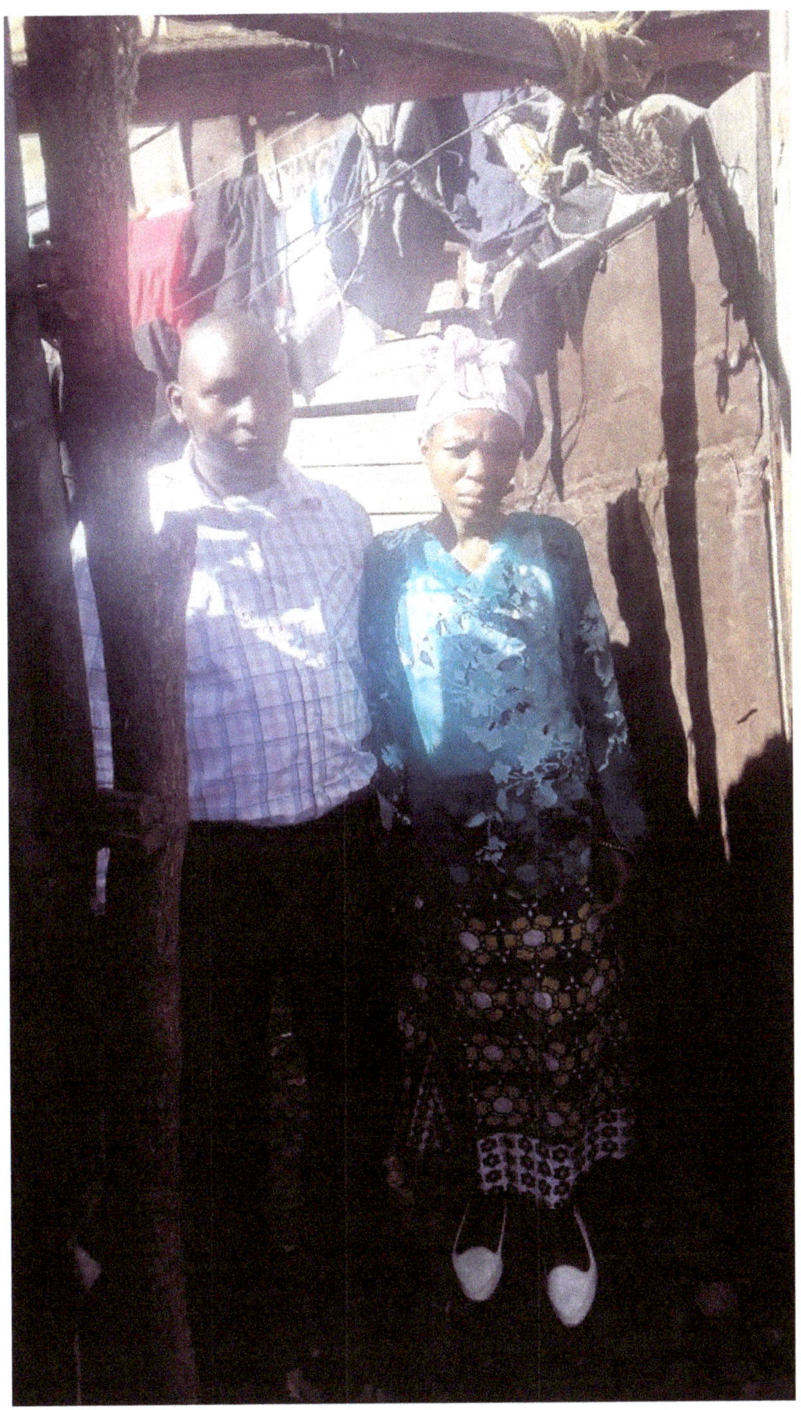

25-04-2018

Dear, friends;

Hello, My name is John Omwena Nyavuto a 6 years-old-boy at St. Tabitha Orthodox Orphanage church and school in Middle class.

I respect the people around me and wishing to go far in my education and become a doctor. Requesting you for more support. Thank you.

Yours Sincerely.
John Omwena

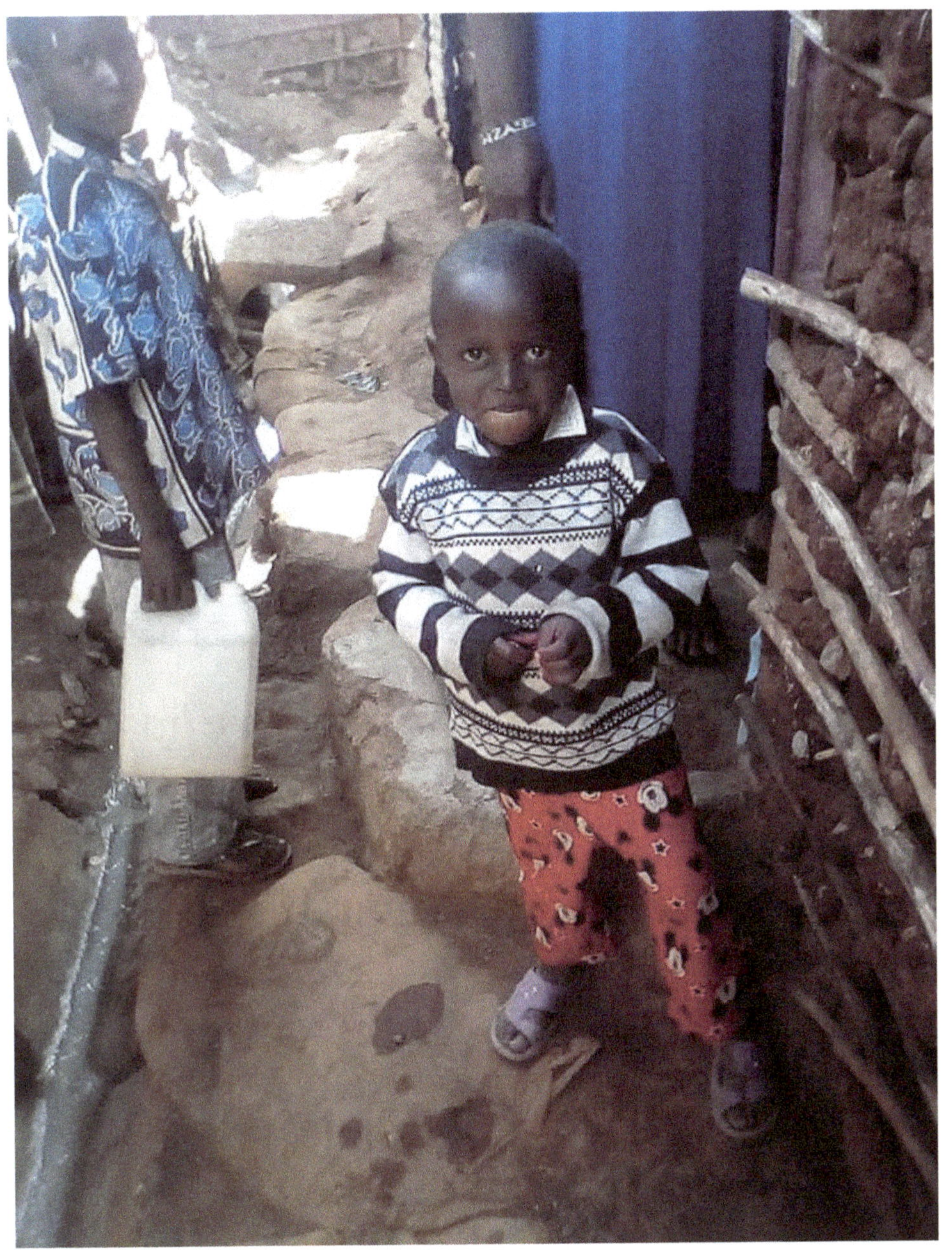

Some women in the area visit to help care for the orphans from time to time.

It is also important for their children to know there is somewhere they can go for help if anything should ever happen to them.

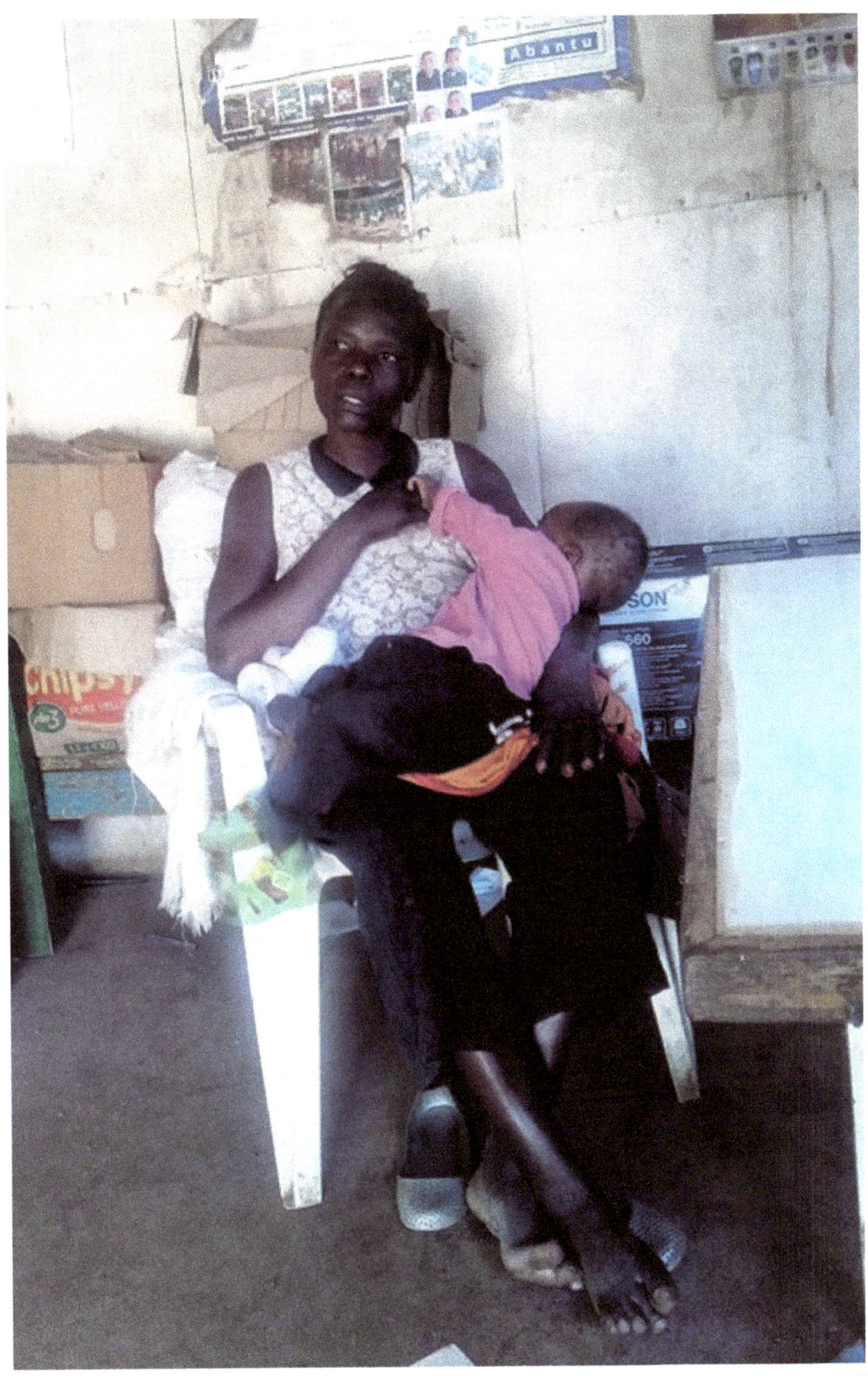
Abantu

25/4/2018

Dear friends;

Hello, my name is Grace Eleni Kipesa. Am 11 years old girl at St. Tabitha Orthodox ophanage church and school - in Class Six.

I scored the following marks in the following subjects:

1. Math - 50 %

2. English - 74 %

3. Kiswahili - 76 %

4. Science - 72 %

5. Social Studies / C.R.E - 69 %

But i will put more effort next term to score high marks.

I respect the people around me and wishing to go for in my education and became a nurse. Requesting you for more support. Thank you.

Yours sincerely,

Grace Eleni Lipesa.

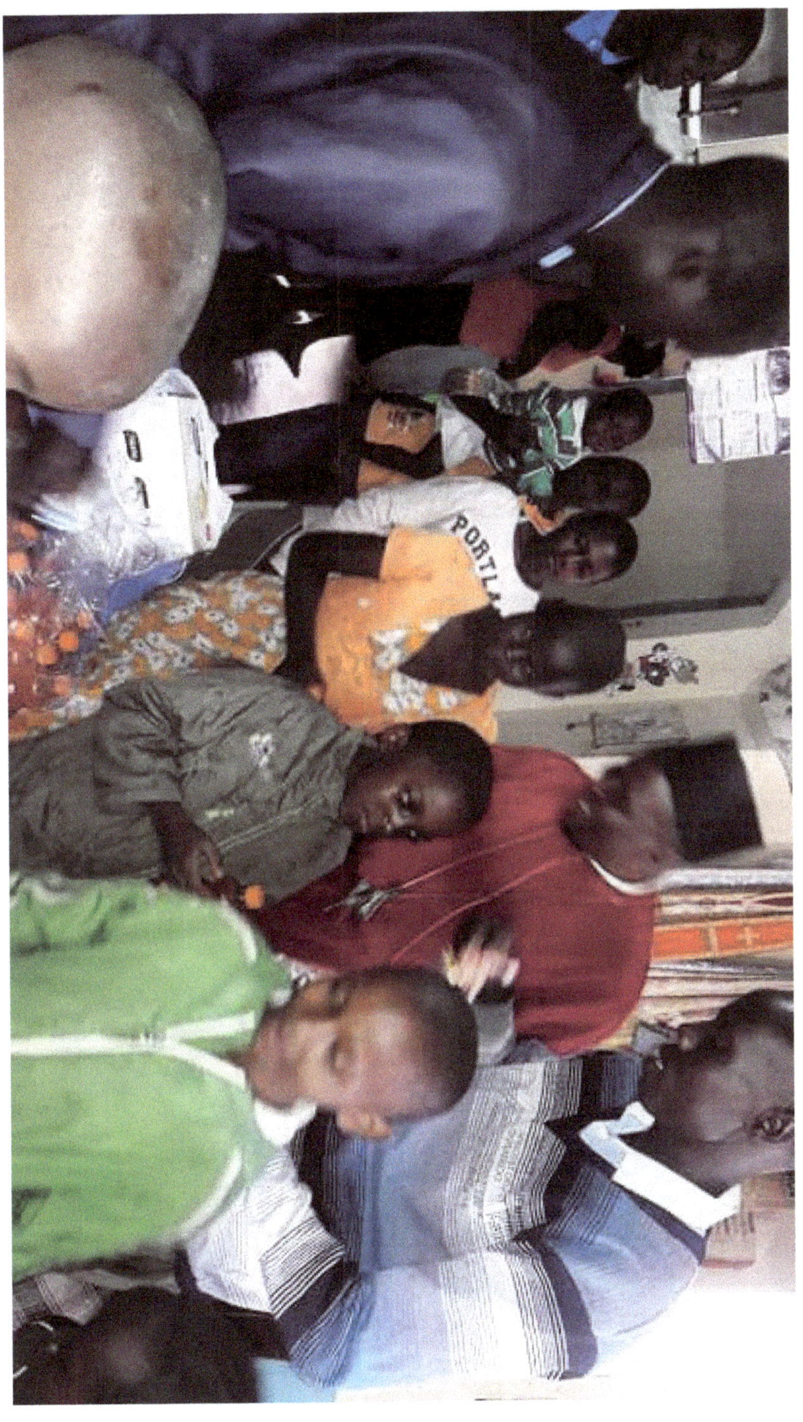

To feed so many orphans, we need to buy a lot of food every month.

Our food budget is $500 per month for everyone at Saint Tabitha's House.

We always appreciate it when visitors help us or when we receive unexpected donations.

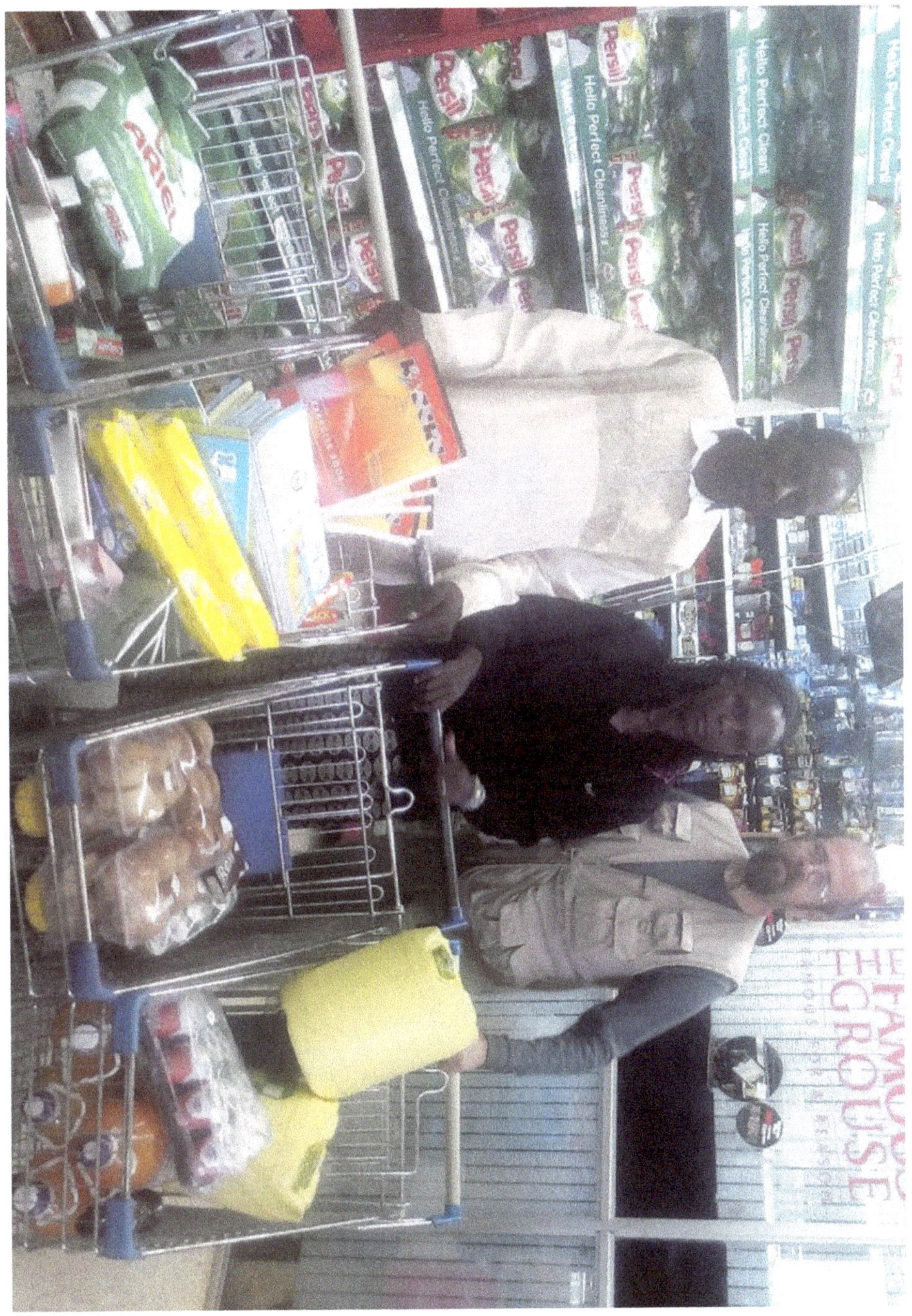
Persil
Hello Perfect Cleanliness
ARIEL
THE FAMOUS GROUSE

Dear Friends

Hello my name is Demetrios Chemwama
13 years old boy at St Tabitha orthodox orphanage
Church and school is class 7

I respect the people around me and wishing
to go far in my education and become
police. Requesting you for more suppot

Thank you
yours sincerely
Demetrios Chemwama

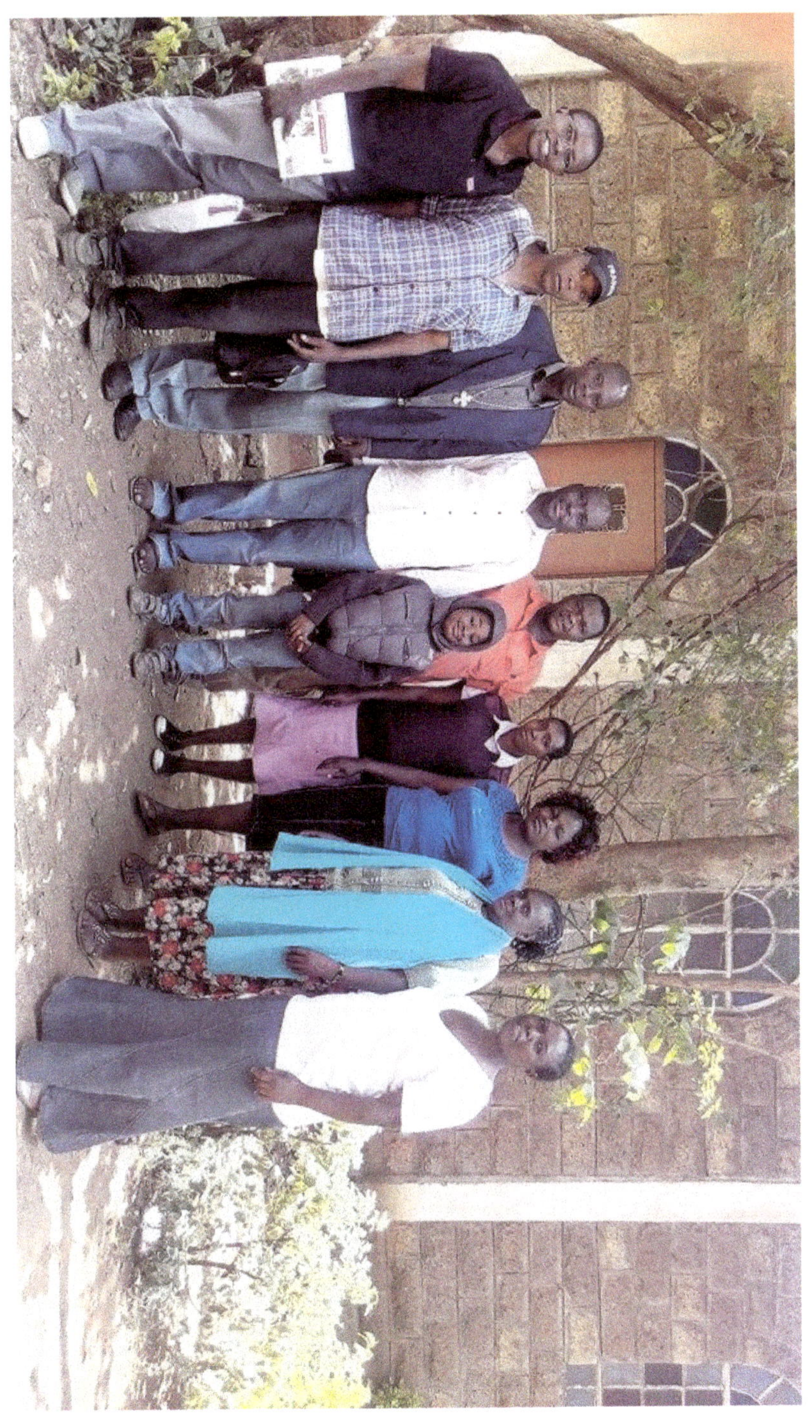

Our Faith

His Grace Bishop Athanasius Akunda was born in Kenya in 1971.

He converted to the Orthodox Christian Faith with his parents and younger siblings when he was eight years old.

He has studied in Kenya, South Africa, India and the United States of America.

Over the years, His Grace has taught several different subjects at various Kenyan high schools.

We at Saint Tabitha's House are very blessed to have His Grace as our protector and guide and we pray for him every day.

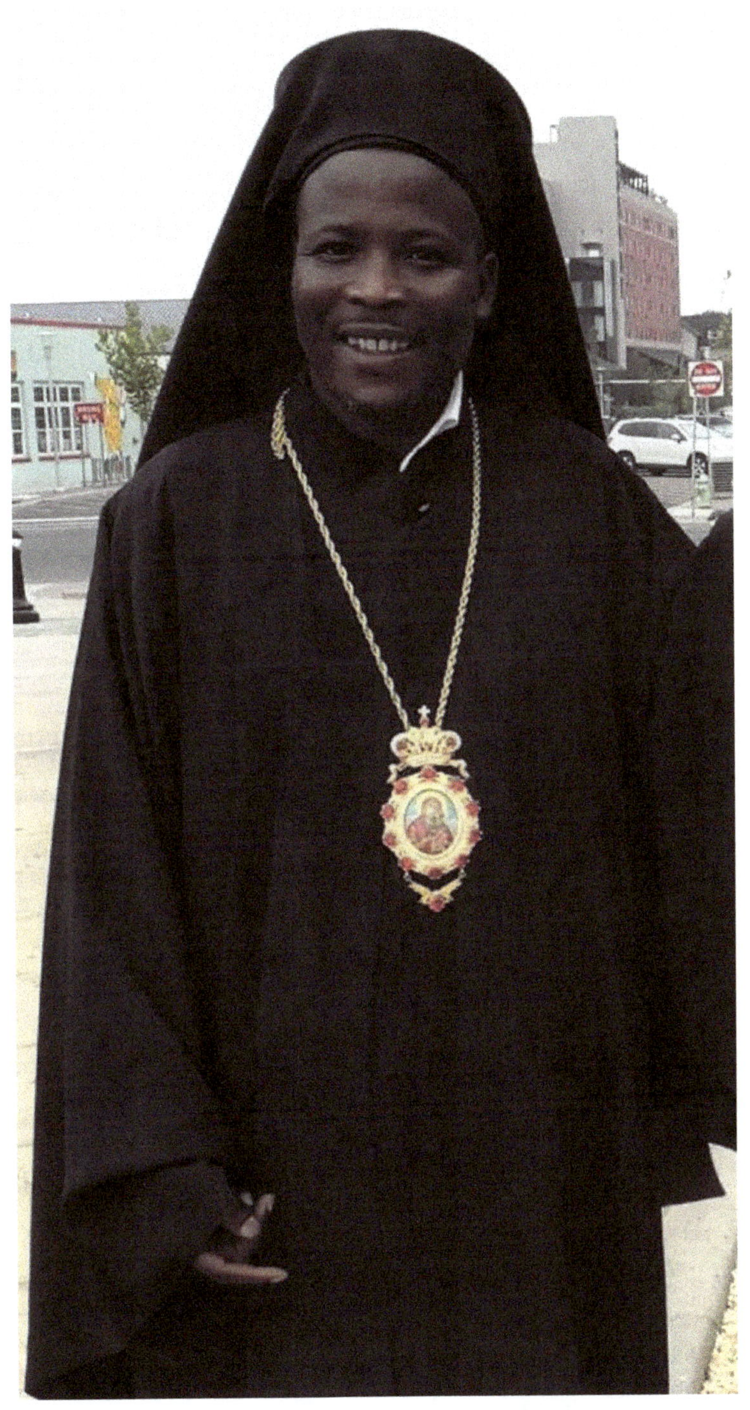

25/4/2018

Dear friends;

Hi! my name is Stanley kamau a 17 - years old - boy at St, Tabitha orphanage. I school at Shirali secondary school in Form 3. and like reading storybooks for my leisure time

Last term I scored the following grades in my 8 subjects
1. MATH - E
2. KISWAHILI - C-
3. ENGLISH - C+
4. CHEMISTRY - D-
5. BIOLOGY - D-
6. GEOGRAPHY - D+
7. CHRISTIAN RELIGIOUS EDUCATION - C+
8. BUSINESS STUDIES - B-

and got amean grade of [D+] but I promise to put more effort and improve my grades and be a successfull person in life

I am a respectfull God fearing boy. I would really want to go far in my education and be a Lecturer. I realy need your support to realize my Dream. Thanks you and may God bless you. Please remember I need your positive reply.

Yours sincerely
Stanley kamau

Replys please - - - -

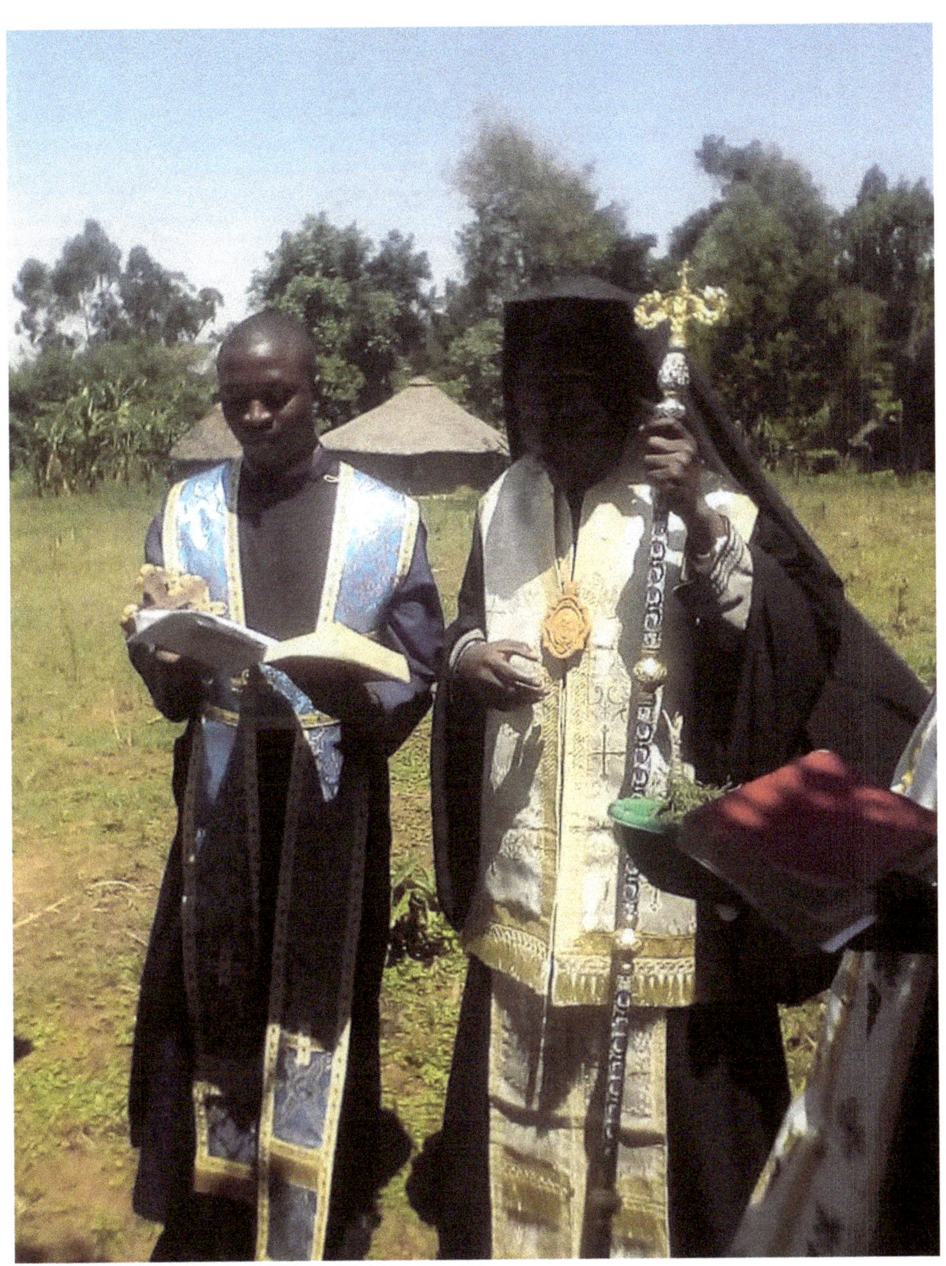

In the Church, only unmarried men may be ordained as Christian bishops.

But the Lord Jesus Christ said that anyone who forsakes having a family for God's sake will receive another family in this life and in the world to come eternal life.

God keeps His promises.

Children are a blessing from the Lord.

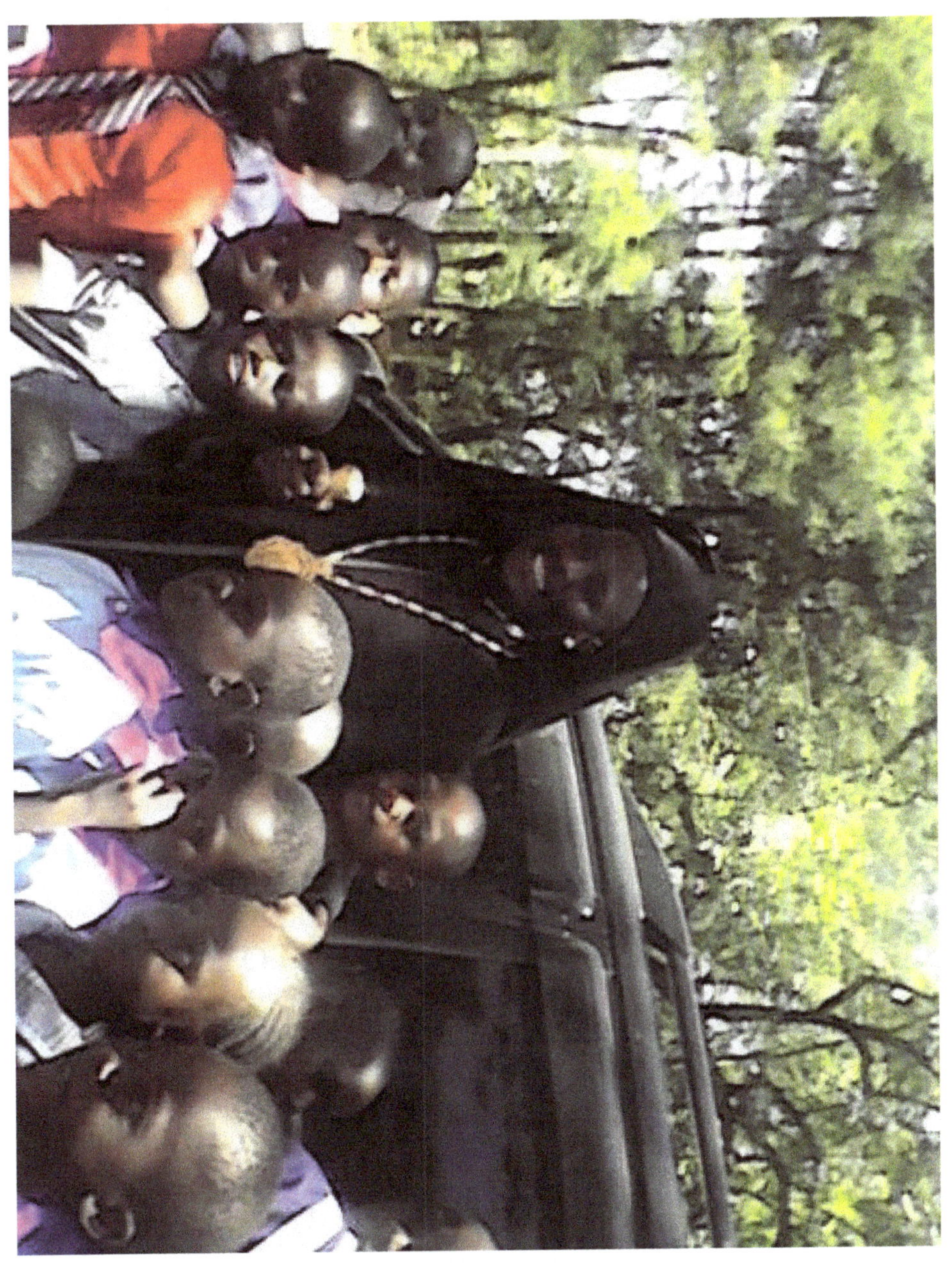

Our priest Father Agapios Habbil Lipesa Omukuba was canonically ordained by His Eminence the Most Reverend Archbishop Makarios the Metropolitan of Kenya.

He is married to Papadia Dorah and together they have 2 sons and 2 daughters of their own.

He founded Saint Tabitha Orphanage in the Kibera slums and remains its director.

Later, we relocated to the Kisumu Diocese because of security issues.

He also continues to fulfil his pastoral duties.

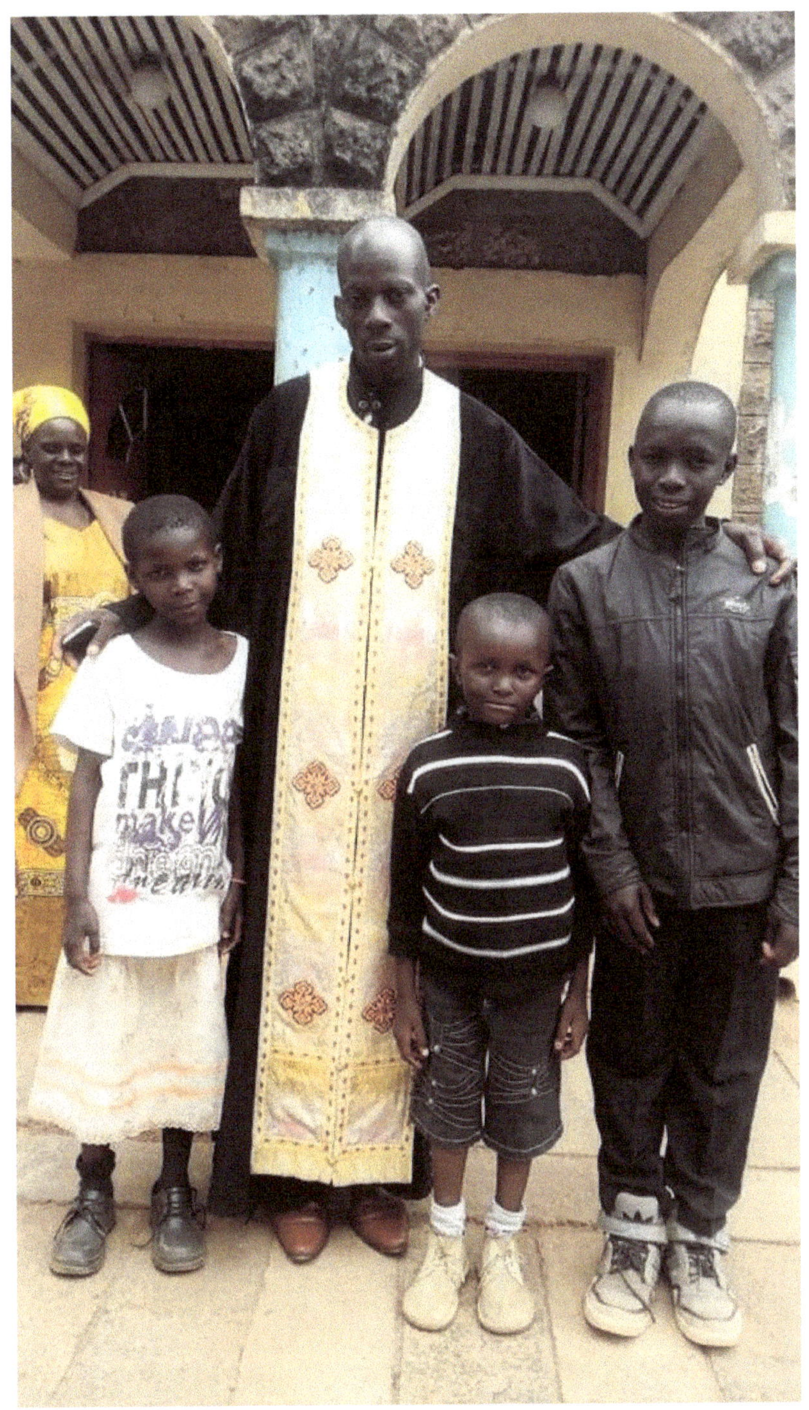

25/4/2018

Dear, friends

Hello, My name is James Keguro
19 years old boy at St. Tabitha
orthodox church and school in
class 8. I respect the people
around me and wishing to
go far in my education
and become an Engineak.
requsting you for more
support thank you.
Yours sintereIy.
James Keguro.

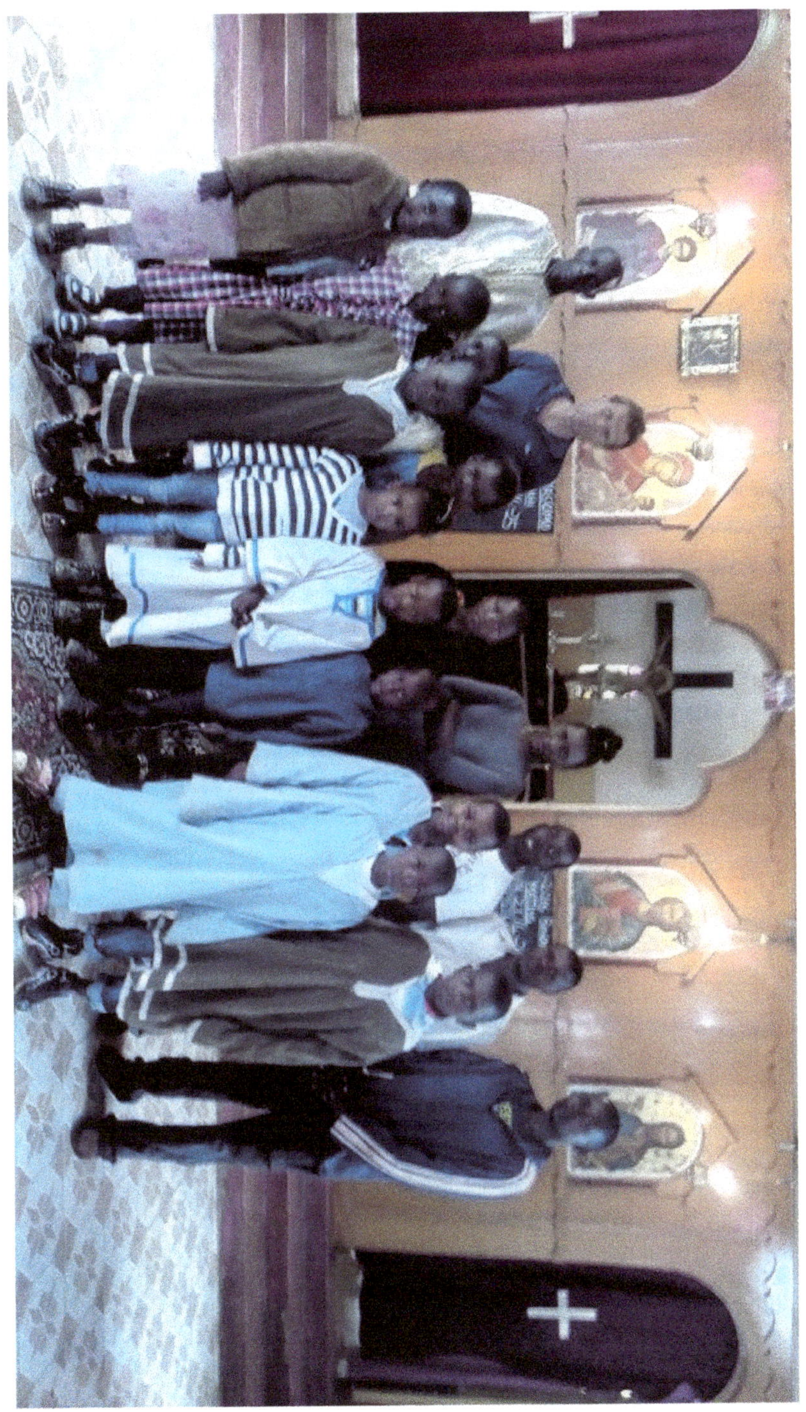

Father Agapios was himself raised in a poor area of Kenya.

His parents could not afford his high school education fees until someone in the Church offered to pay them for him.

When he was studying in the seminary, he asked Archbishop Seraphim if he would permit him to give the seminarian's leftover food to the poor children who attended his Sunday school classes.

He decided to start our orphanage to help children who had no hope.

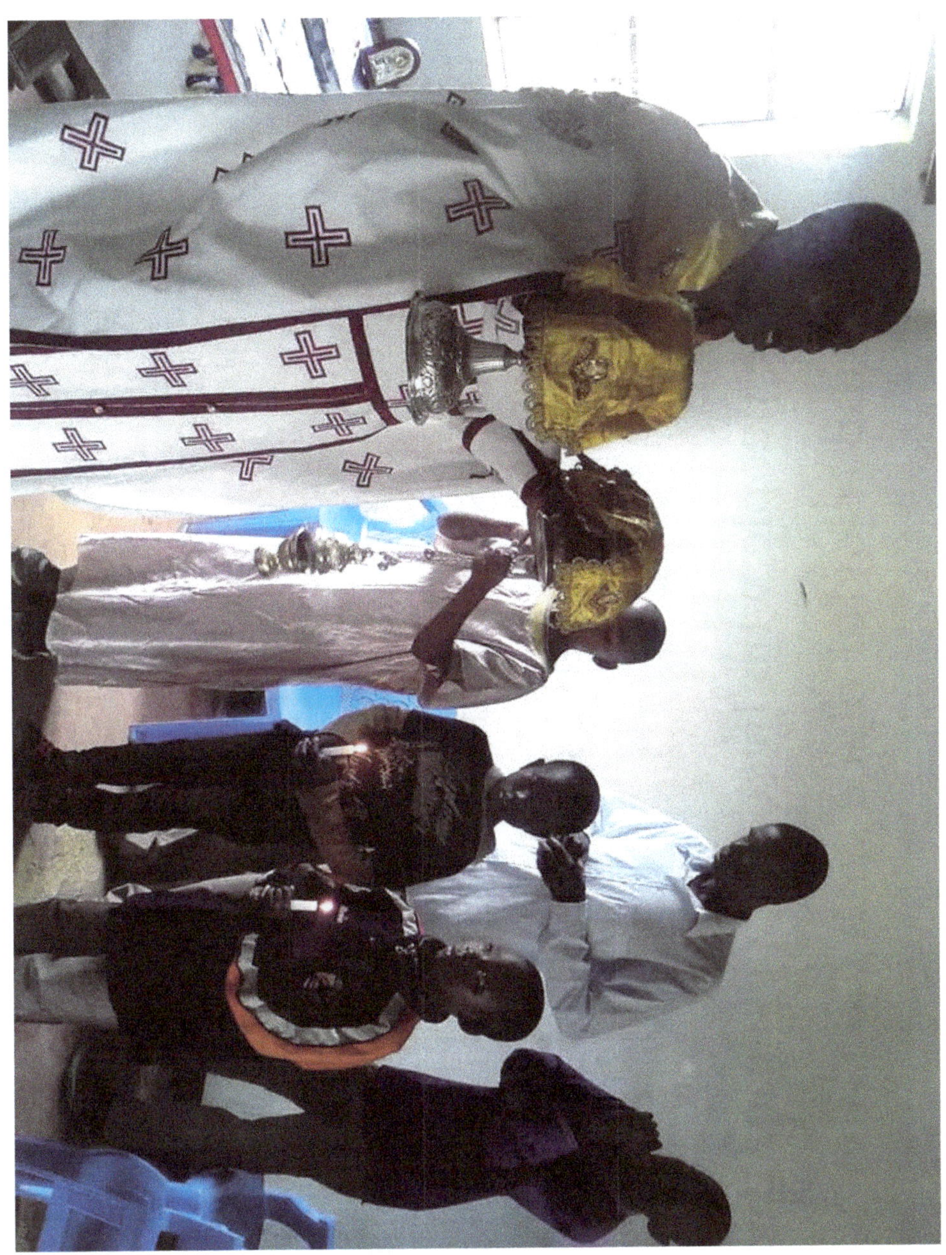

Many people come to worship the Lord in the church from lots of different places.

Inside the church there are icons of our Lord Jesus Christ and the saints to remind us that they are our family and we should respect them.

The saints are people who lived holy lives in this world and found a joyful place with God above.

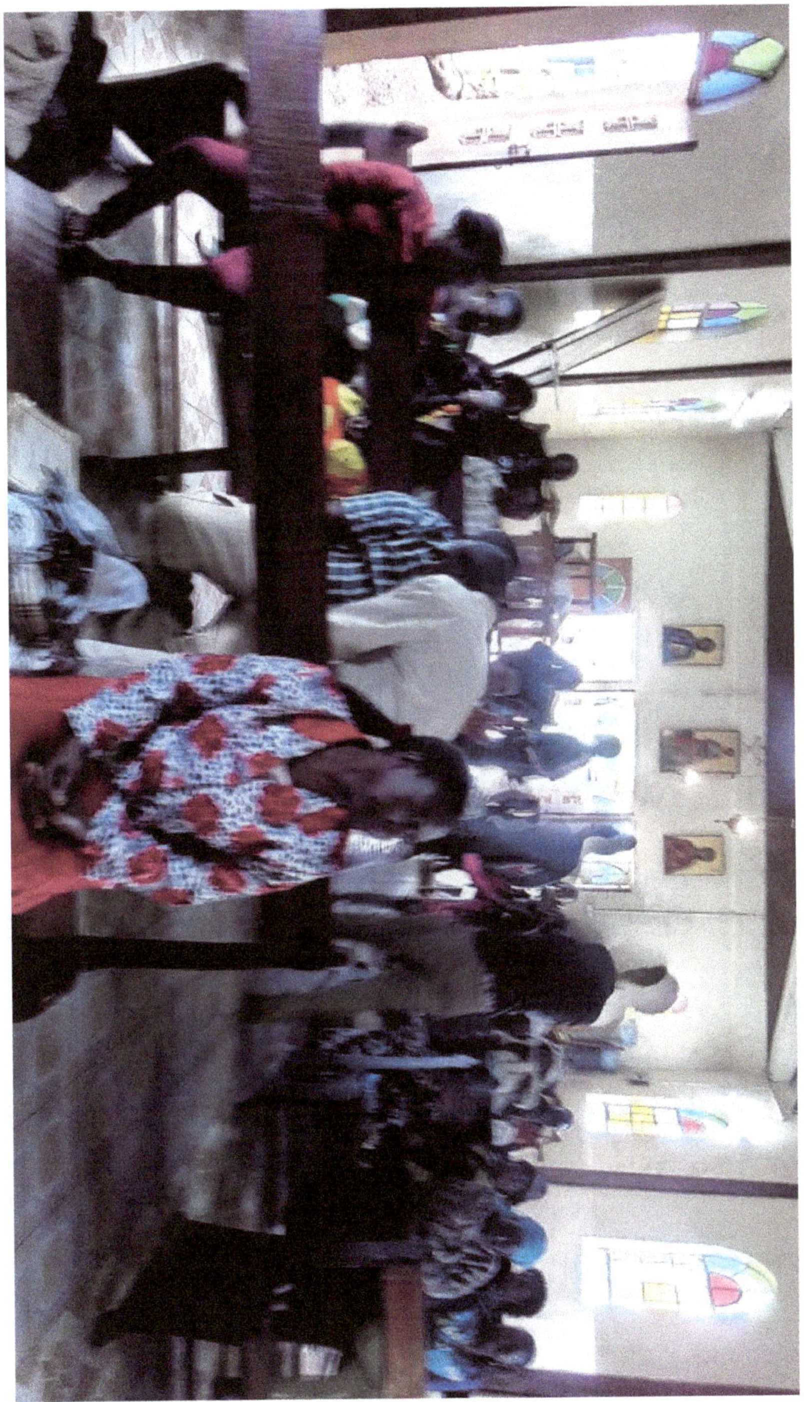

Even young children are taught to hold lighted candles.

The fire reminds us of the Light of God.

It provides warmth and helps us to see.

But we must learn early on to respect the flame because it can burn us too unless we are careful.

So too, we must respect the mighty Lord God who provides us with so many blessings.

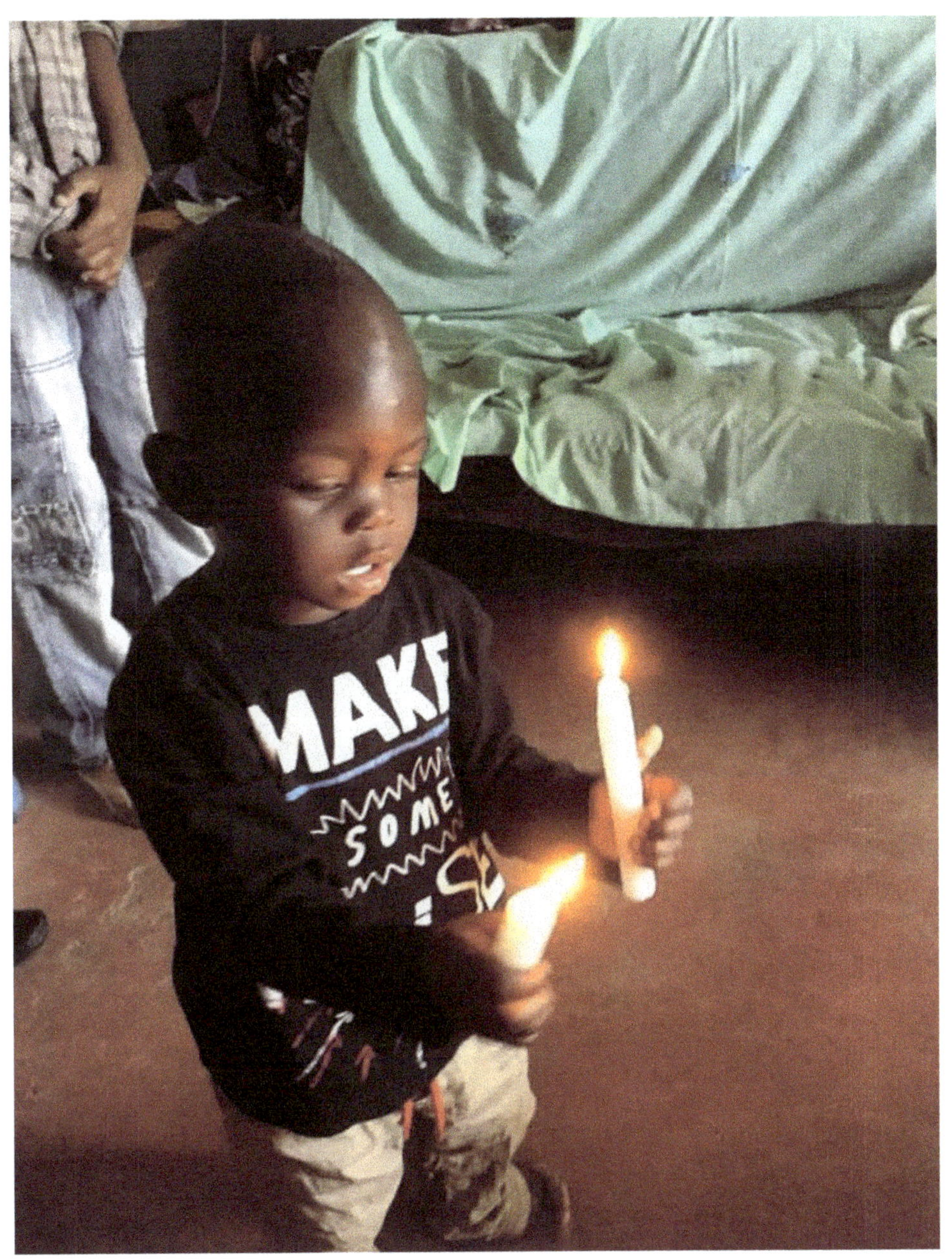
SOME

Dear, Friends; 25/4/2018

Hello, My name is Scholasticah Wangui a 10-years-old-girl at St.Tabitha Orthodox orphanage church and school in Class 5.

I respect the people around me and wishing to go far in my education and become a doctor. Requesting you for more support. Thank you.

Yours Sincerely.
Scholasticah Wangui

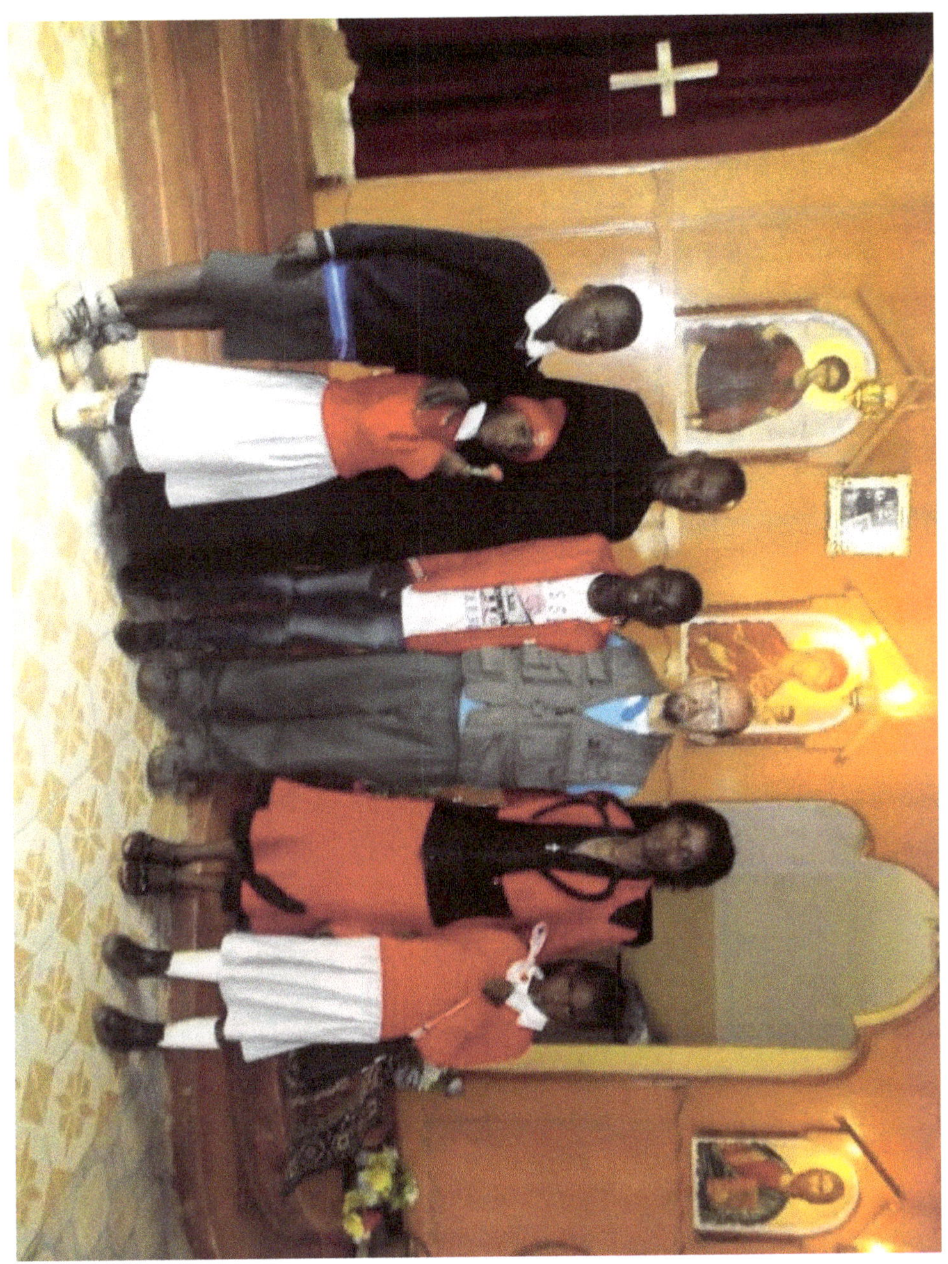

Even in the midst of all our struggles
we can still find time to take photographs
of ourselves together.

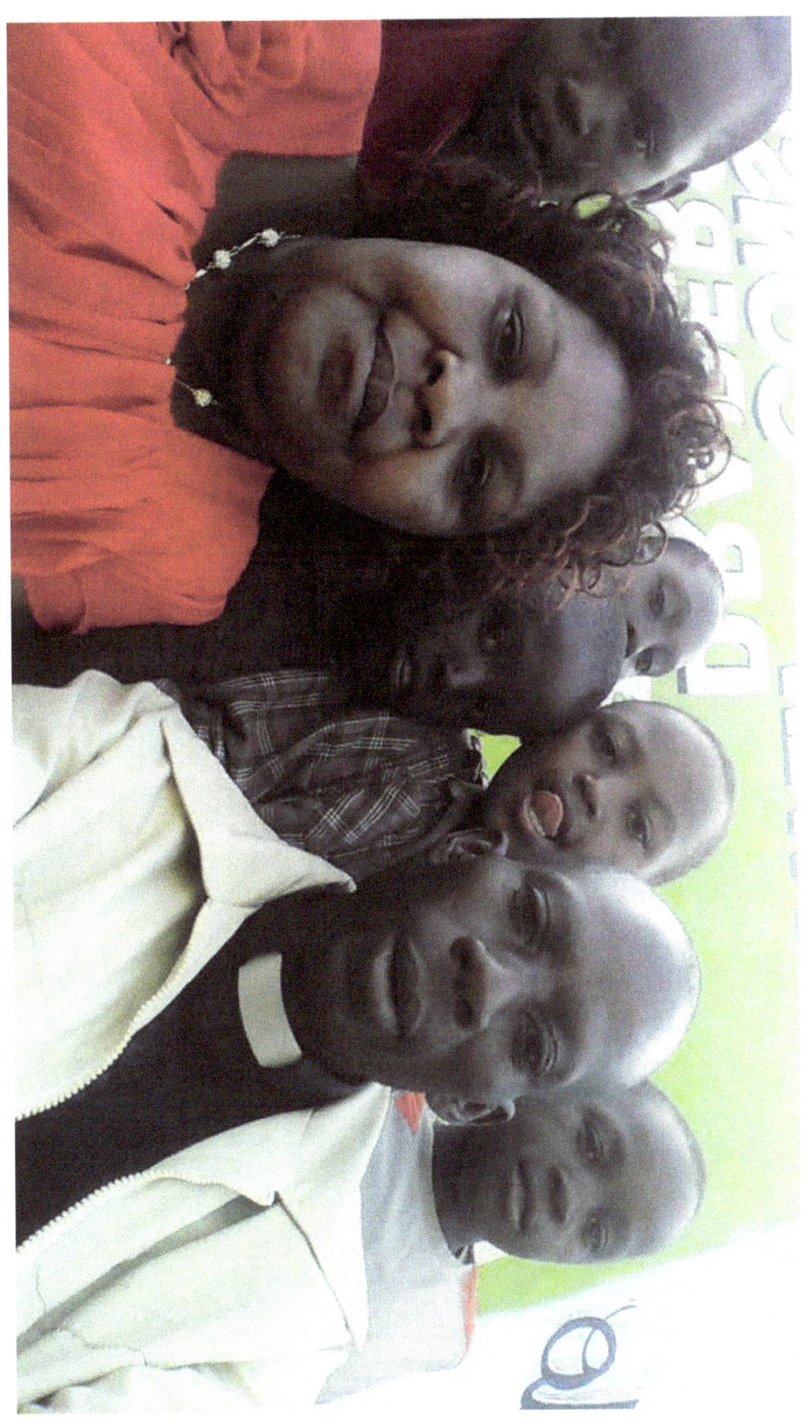

Our Home

Dear, friends 22/6/201

Hello, my name is princess Mwenje a 6 years old girl at ST. TabiTha orthodox orphange church and school in Baby Class.

I respect The people around me and wishing to go far in my education and become a teacher. Requesting you for more suppart thank

yours sinceroly

princess Mwenje

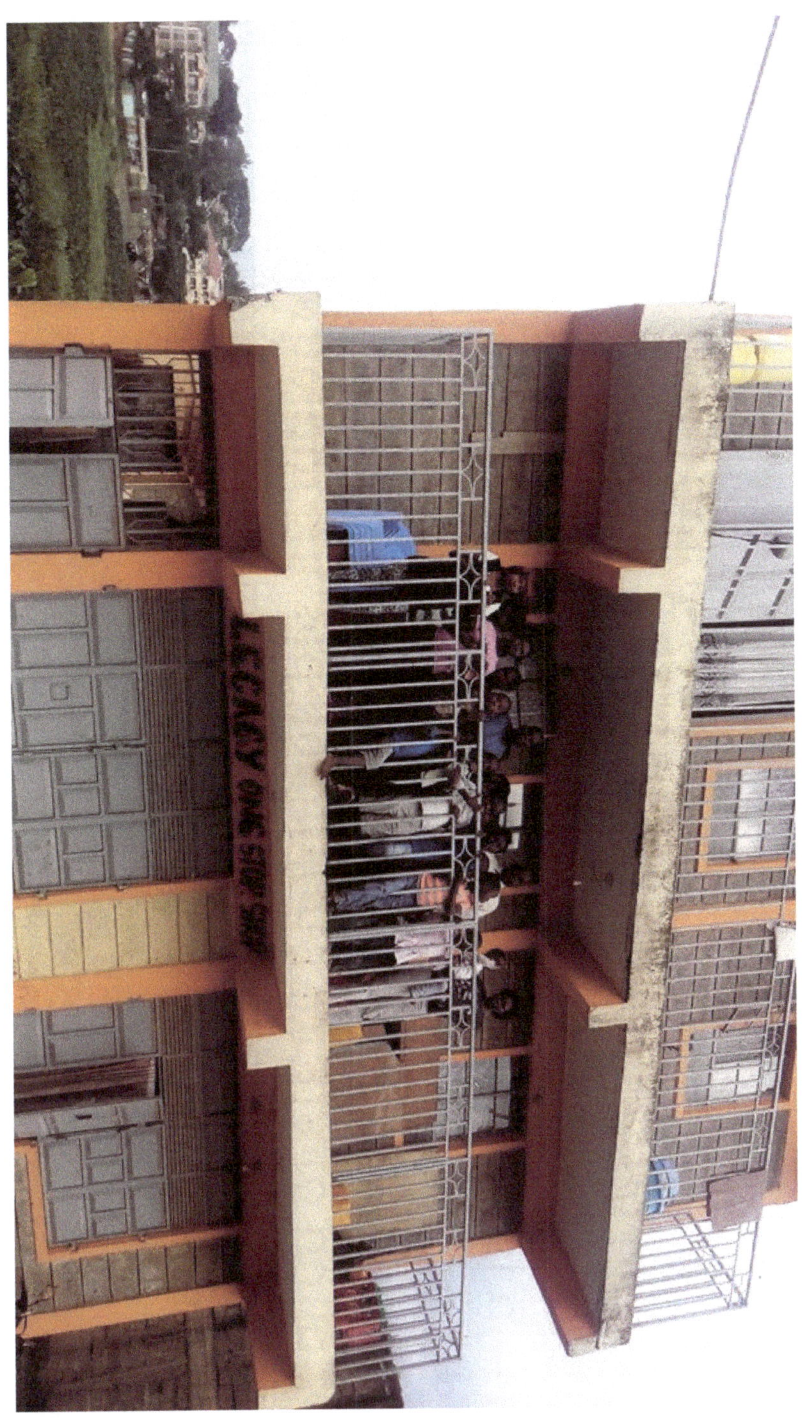
LEGACY ONE STOP SHOP

With the support of His Grace Bishop Athanasius Akunda of Kisumu and all Western Kenya, Chrys Anthe purchased some land for us to build and expand on.

It took a long time to find an affordable parcel of land but thanks to God who provides we were able to find one in a good place.

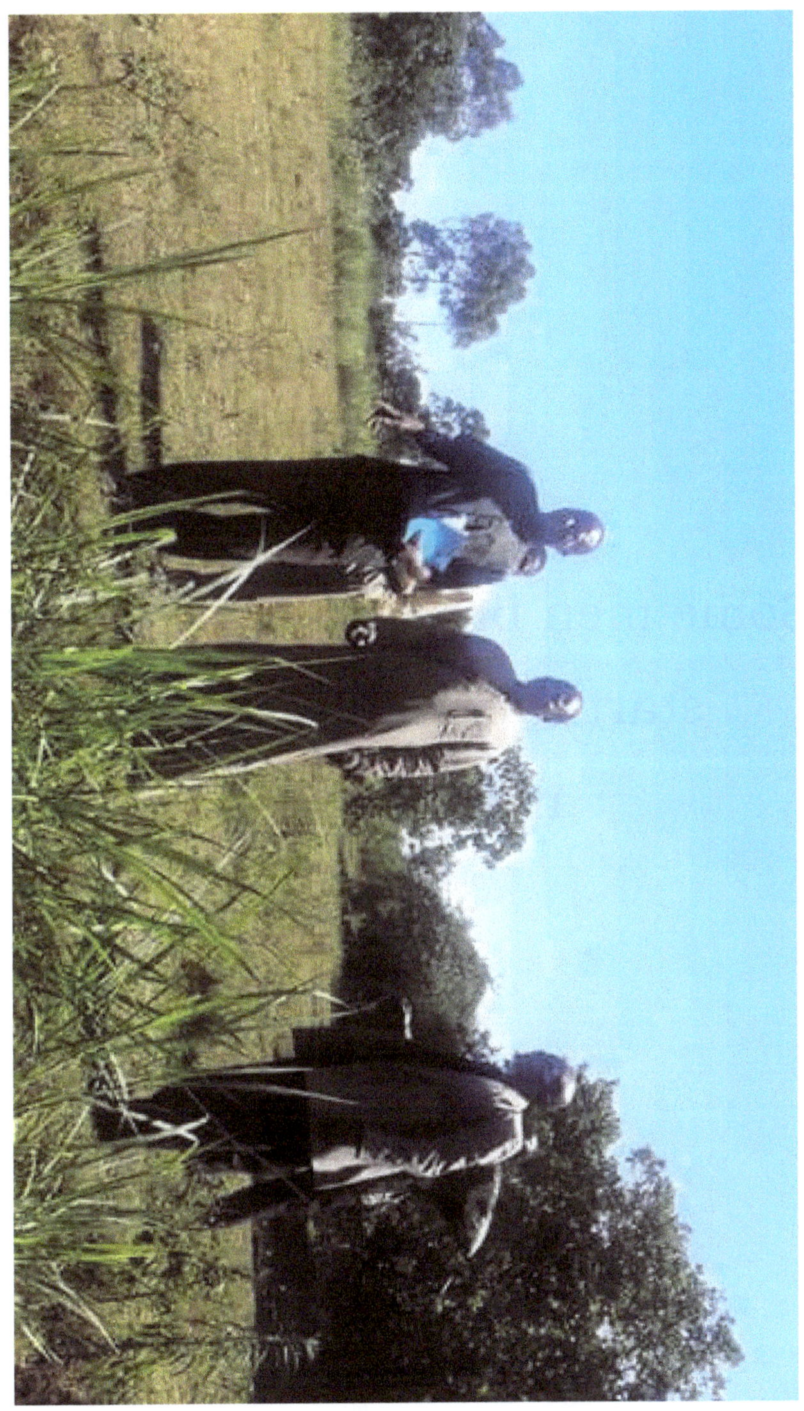

Some men brought wood to help start the building at our new location.

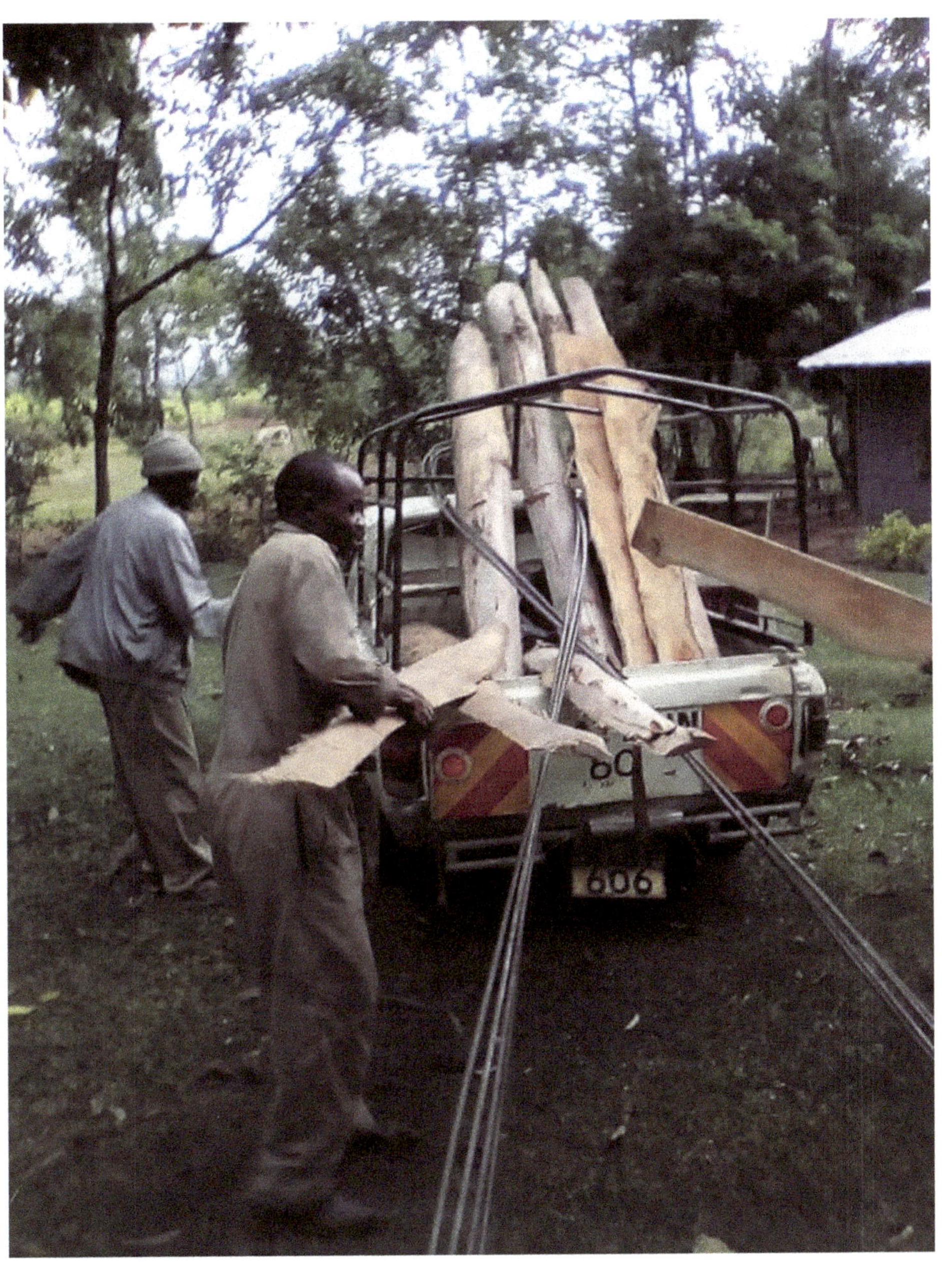
606

The beams of wood were so long they could be seen while sitting in the front seats of the car.

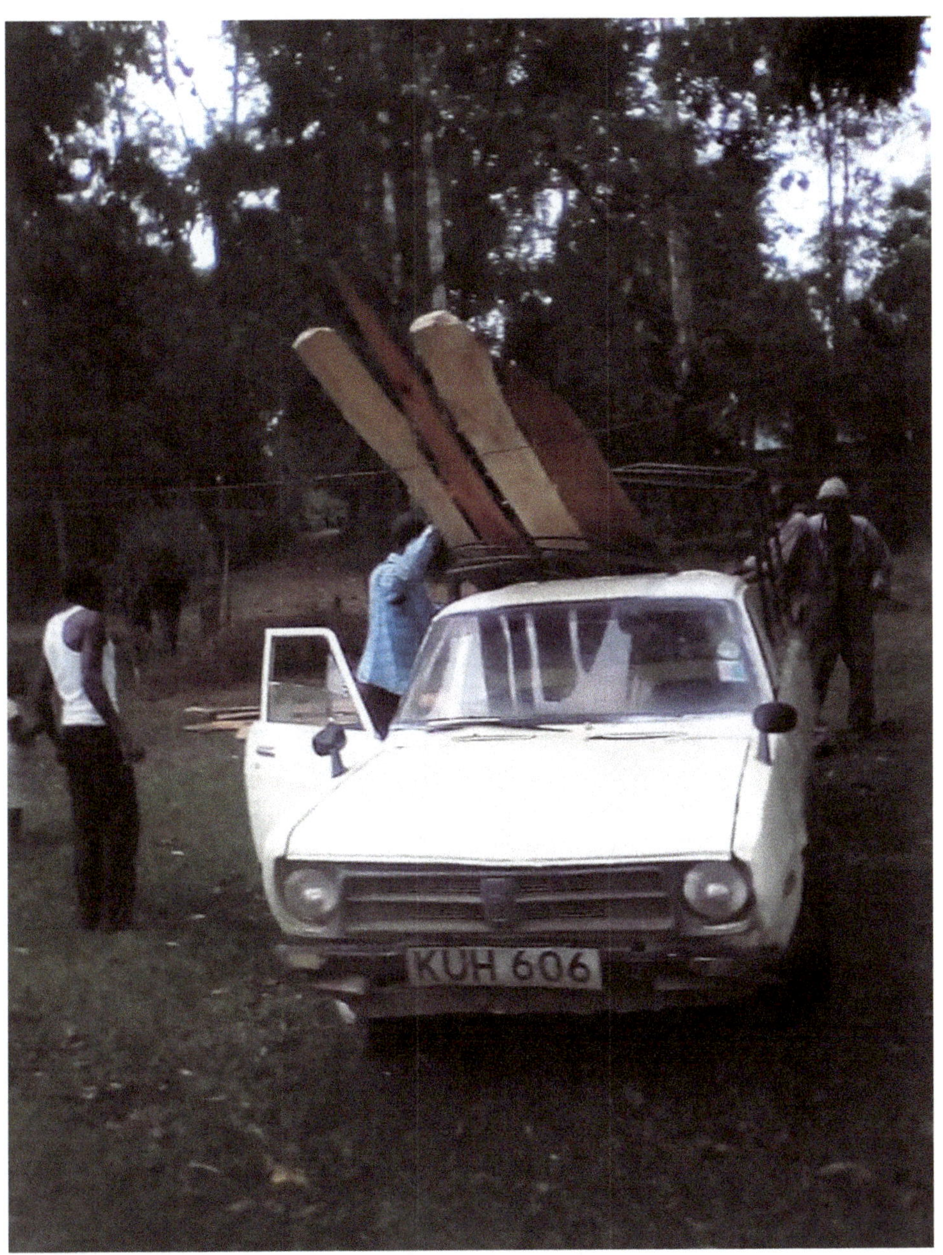
KUH 606

Now we keep some animals at Saint Tabitha's House too.

We have a cow, 4 pigs and 15 chickens.

The cow provides milk and the chickens lay tasty eggs for us all to eat and enjoy.

This helps keep the cost of food to less than $20 per child per month.

But there are still some months when we struggle to afford enough food for all of us to eat.

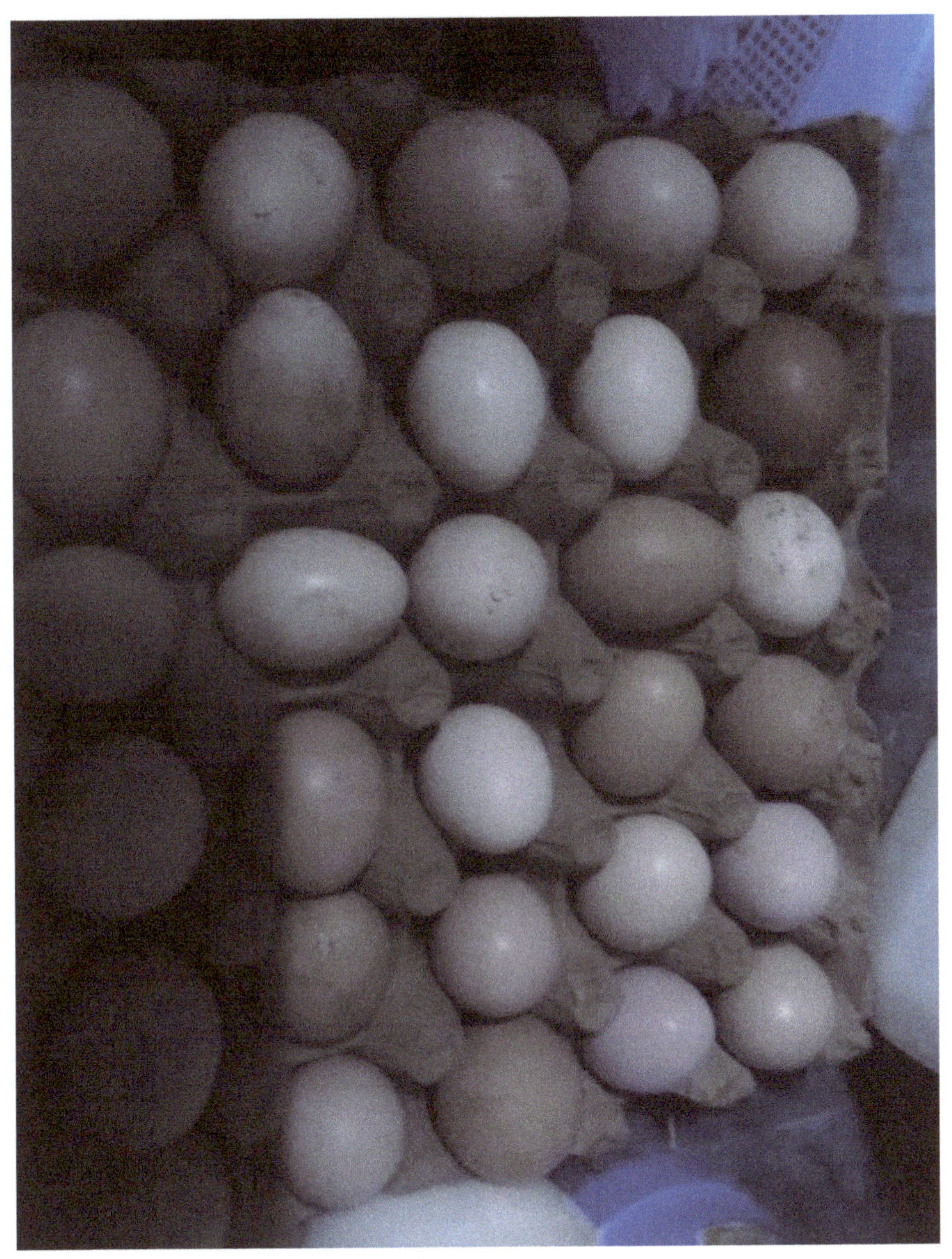

At our new home, we even have a tractor!

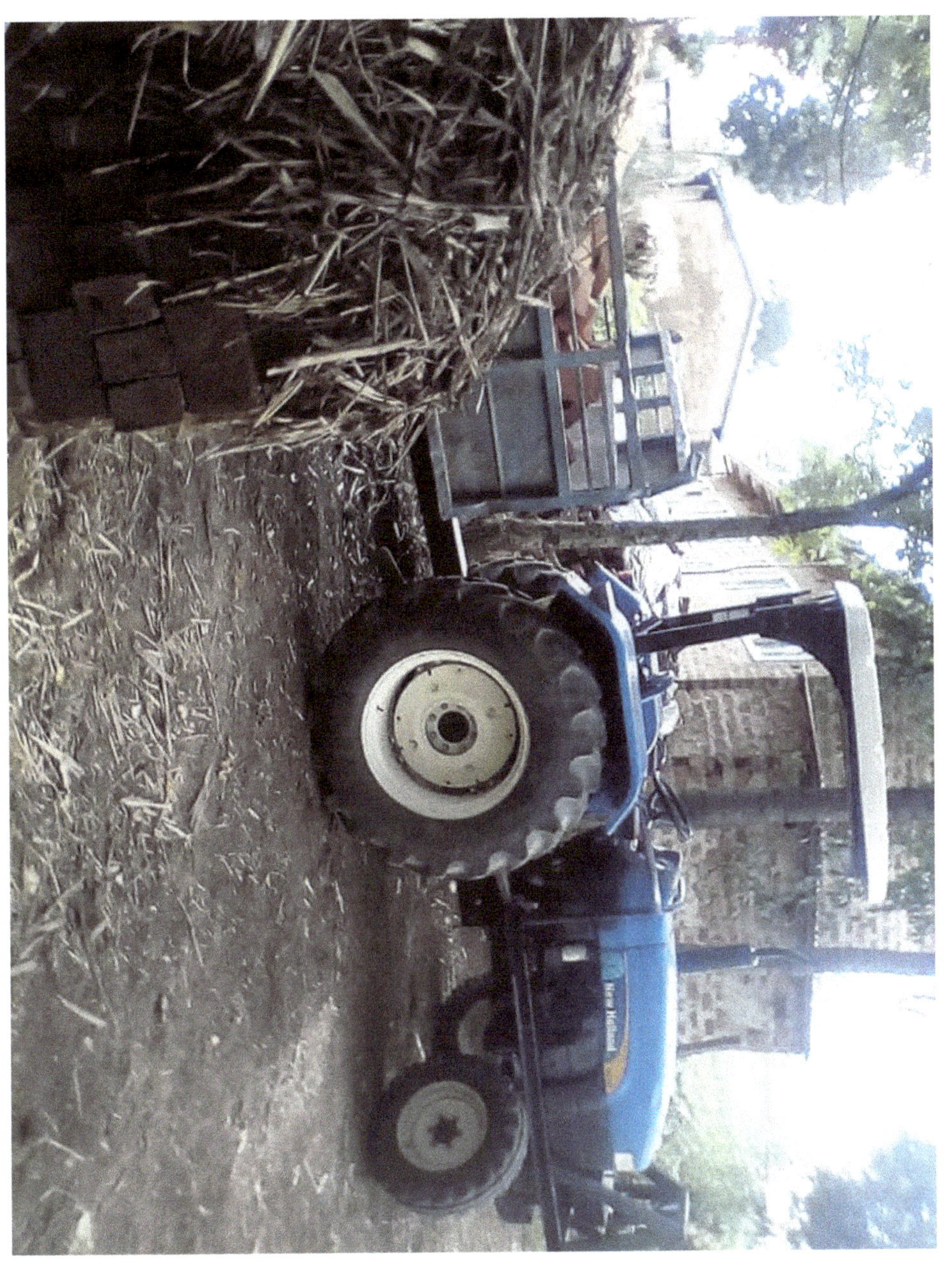
New Holland

25/4/2018

Dear Friends

Hi my name is Emmanuel Lipesa a Fifteen year old boy at St. Tabitha Orthodox Orphanage Church and School in Form two at Mbale High School. I have stayed for Four years at the Orphanage.

Last term I scored the following grades in my Subjects;

1) Mathematics
2) English -B+
3) Kiswahili-C+
4) Geography-C
5) Chemistry
6) Physics - C-
7) Biology - B
8) Agriculture - B-
9) Business Studies-C-
10) Christian religious Education C+
11) History - A

The mean grade was B but i will put more effort next term to score high grades and be a Succesful person in Future. Not forgetting i like playing Football during my leisure time.

I respect the people around me and wishing to go far in my education and become a lawyer. Requesting you for your support. Thank you.

Yours friendly,
Emmanuel Lipesa

Replies please..........

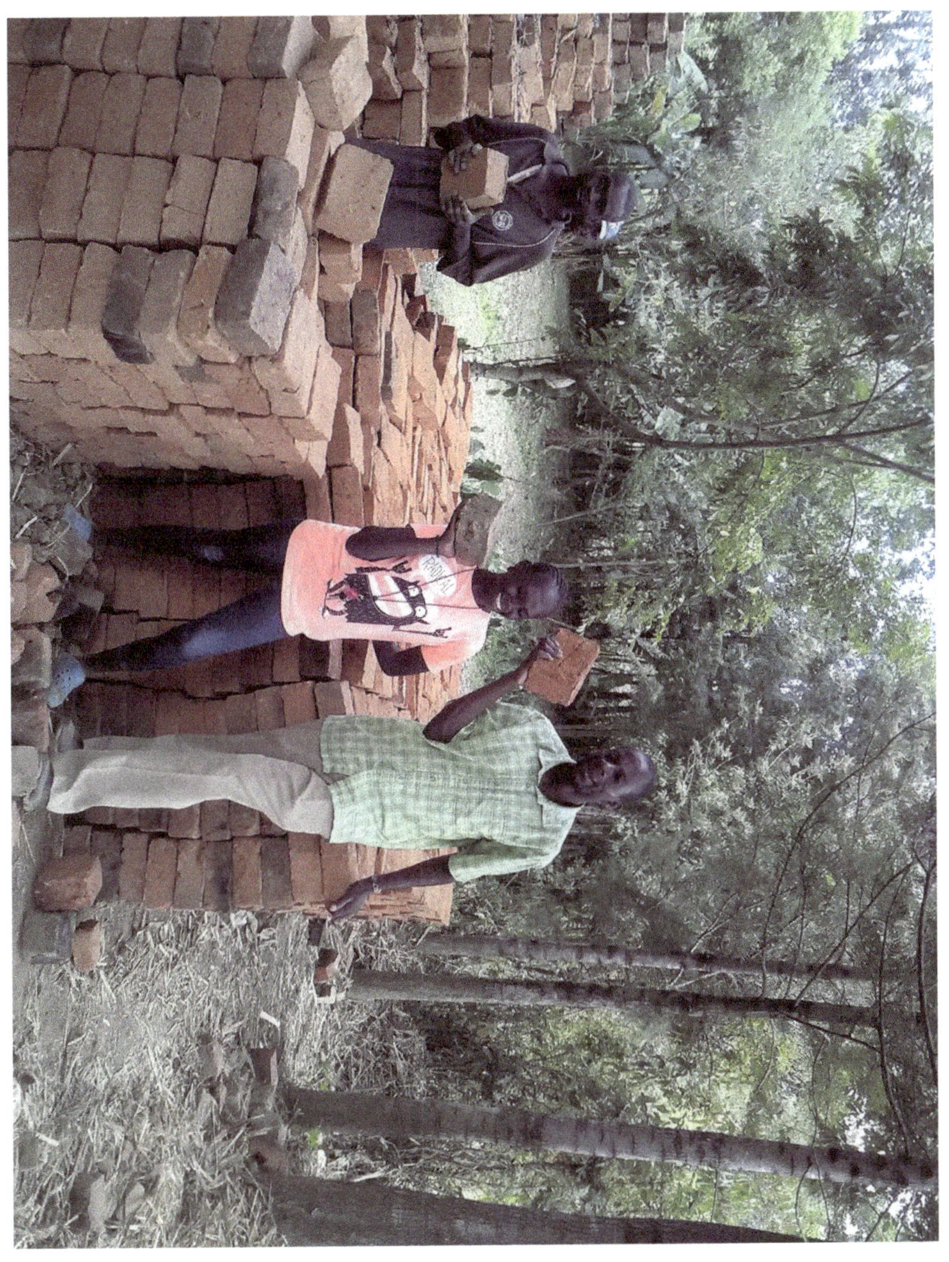

Construction has been financially supported by the Romanian Orthodox Episcopate in Northern Europe.

Their help has made it possible for us to buy many of the building materials we need.

We are very grateful for their support and prayers and pray the Lord may reward them for their loving generosity.

The Lord loves a cheerful giver.

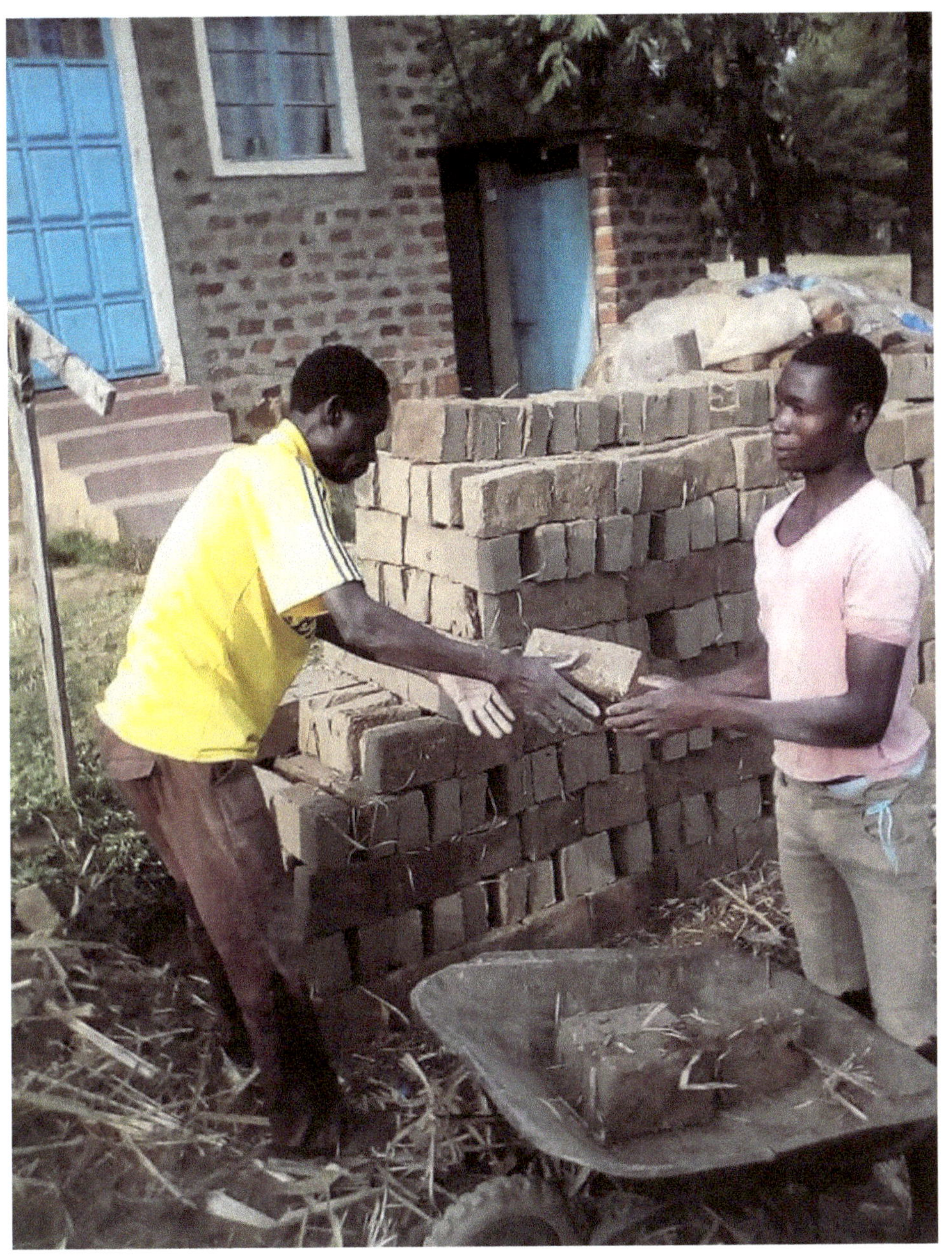

Stacking all the bricks for later use took a long time so we had some rests.

Soon we will have separate washrooms for the boys and the girls built.

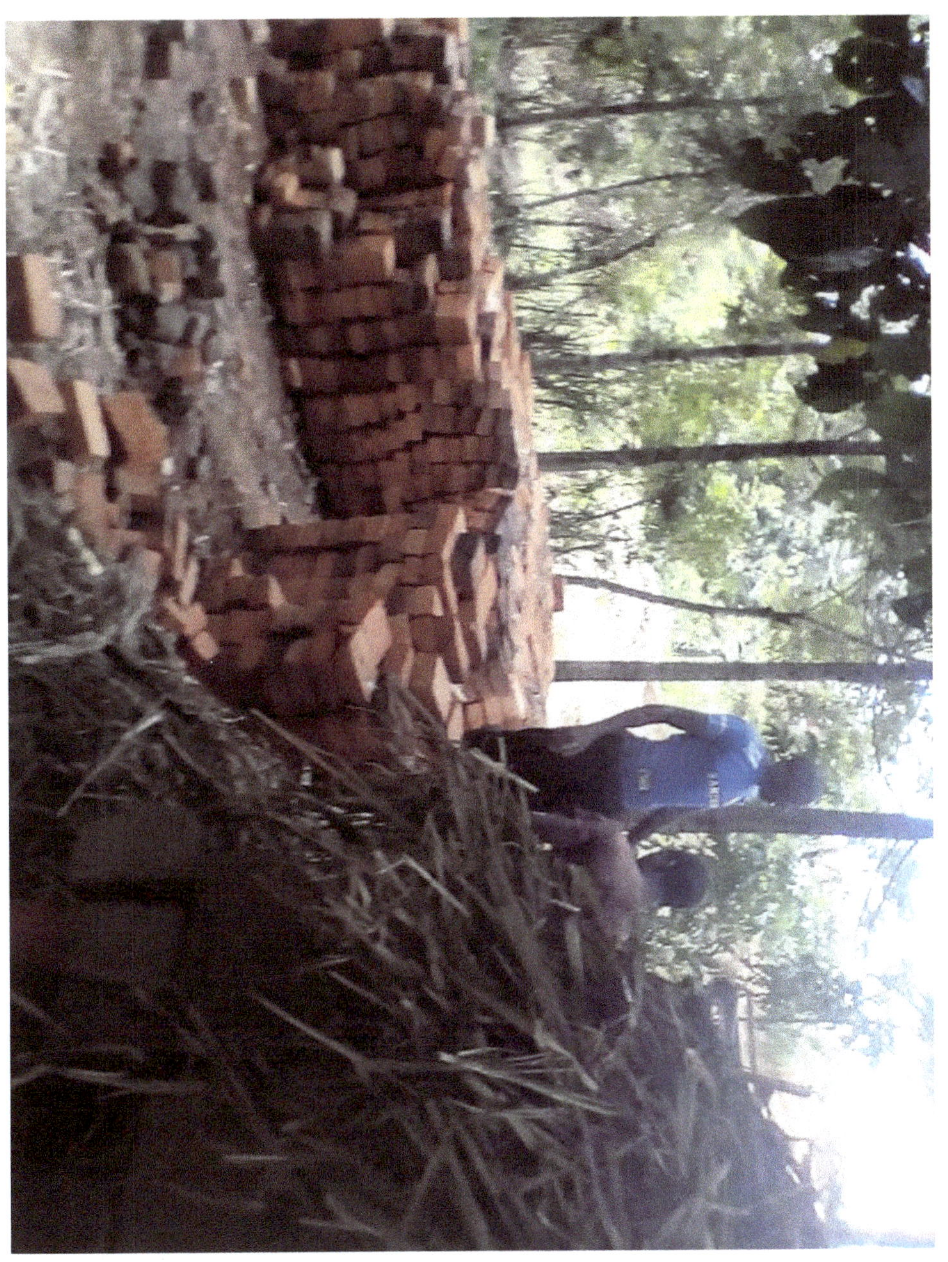

Teamwork helps us build faster than anyone could build by himself without any help.

Maybe one day another book will show what these bricks used for building.

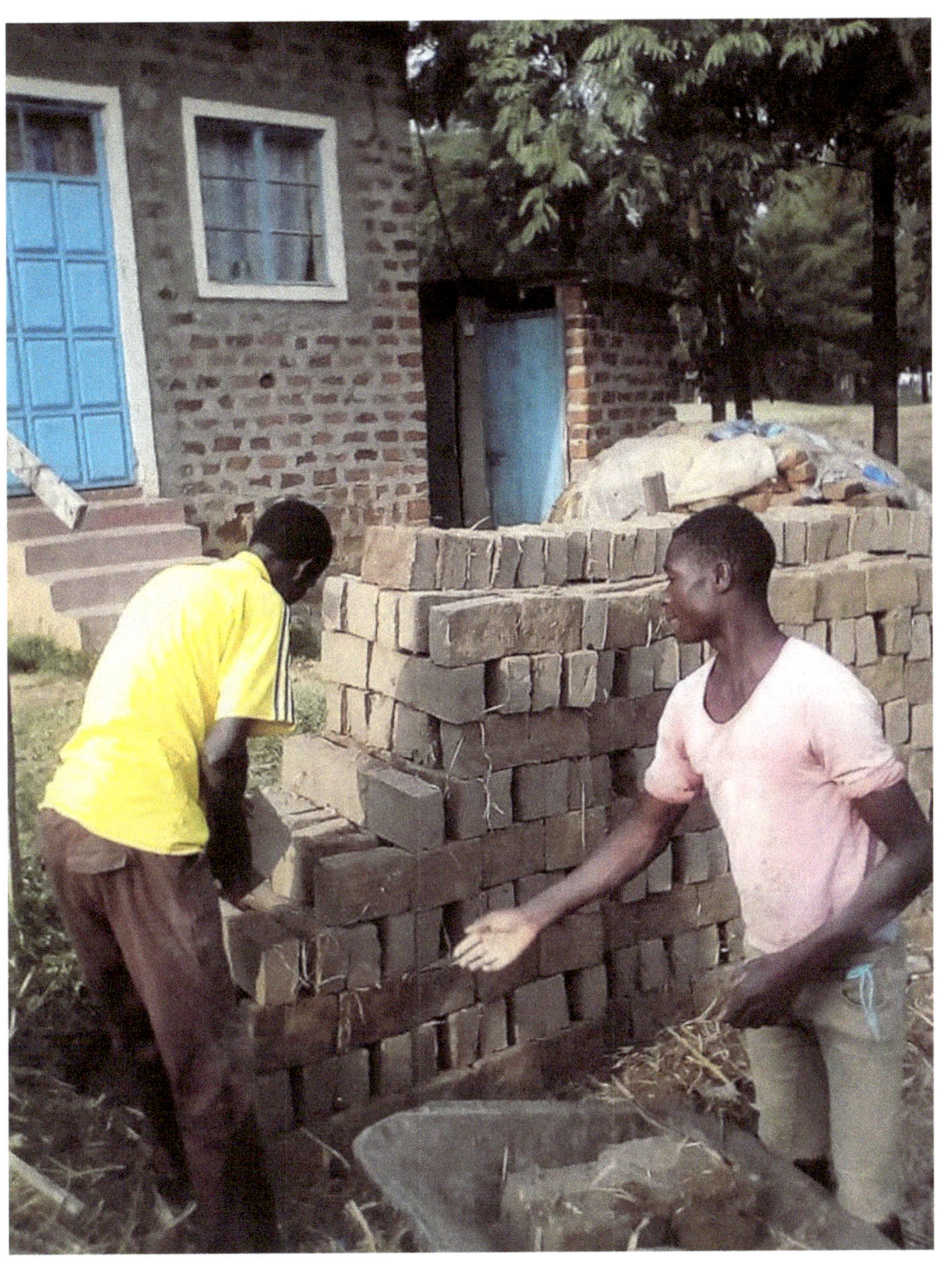

Seeing how far
Saint Tabitha's House has come
since it began makes
everybody smile.

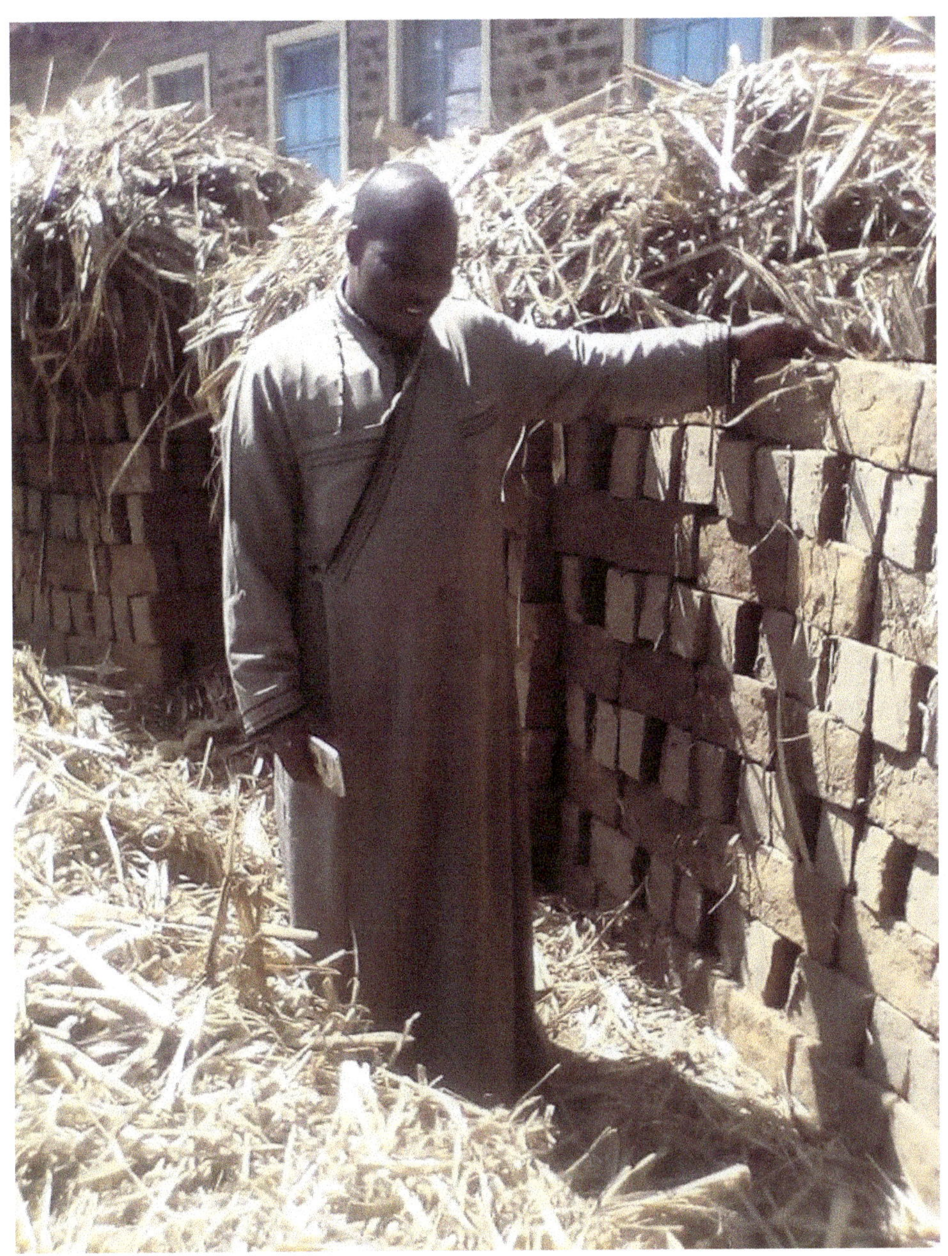

Dear Friend 22/6/2018

Hello, My name is Bruce Mukweyi 10years old boy at St. Tabitha Orphanage Churchar School in Class 4.

I respect the People aroud me and wishing to go far in My education and become a pilct Requesting you for mor support. Thank You.

Yours sincerely,

Bruce Mukweyi

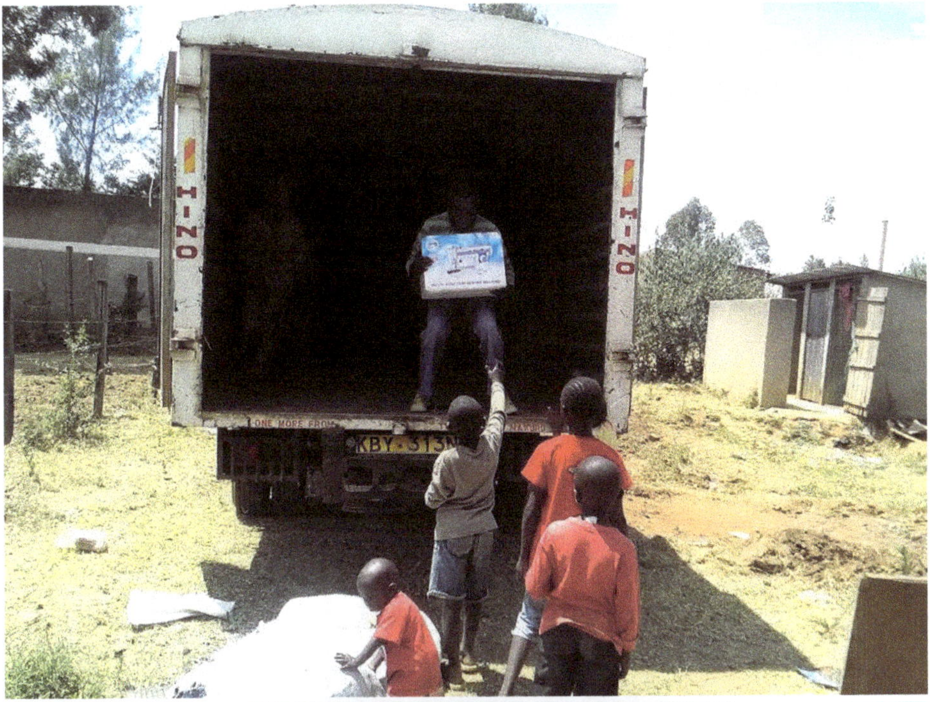
HINO
HINO
KBY 313N

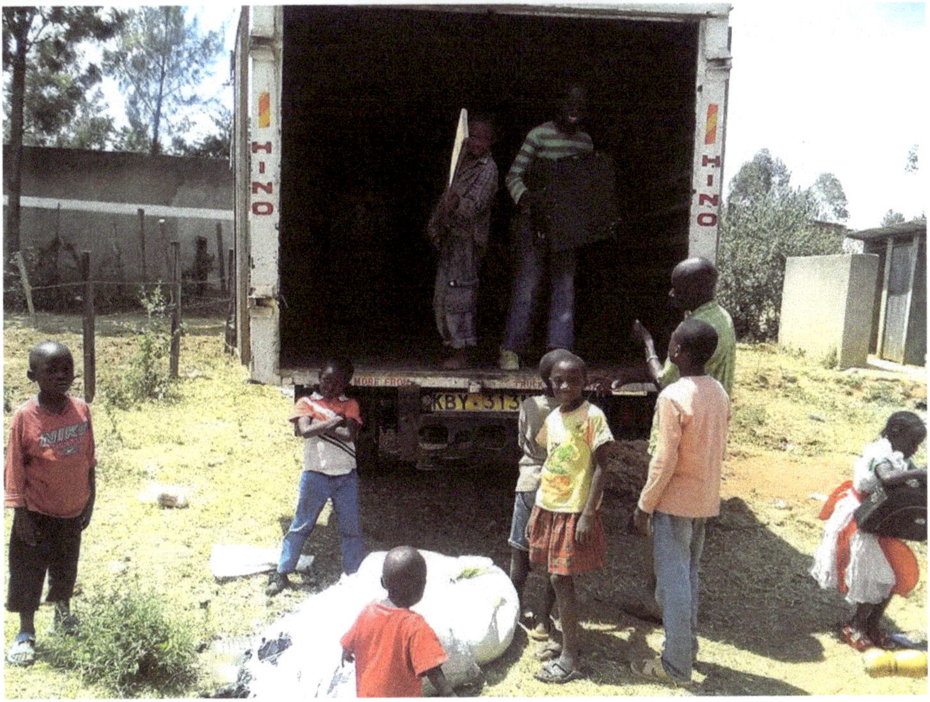
HINO
HINO

We are very thankful for the support of our dear mother Catherine Sofikitis.

Without her assistance, we would not have been able to relocate from the Kibera slums to a safe place.

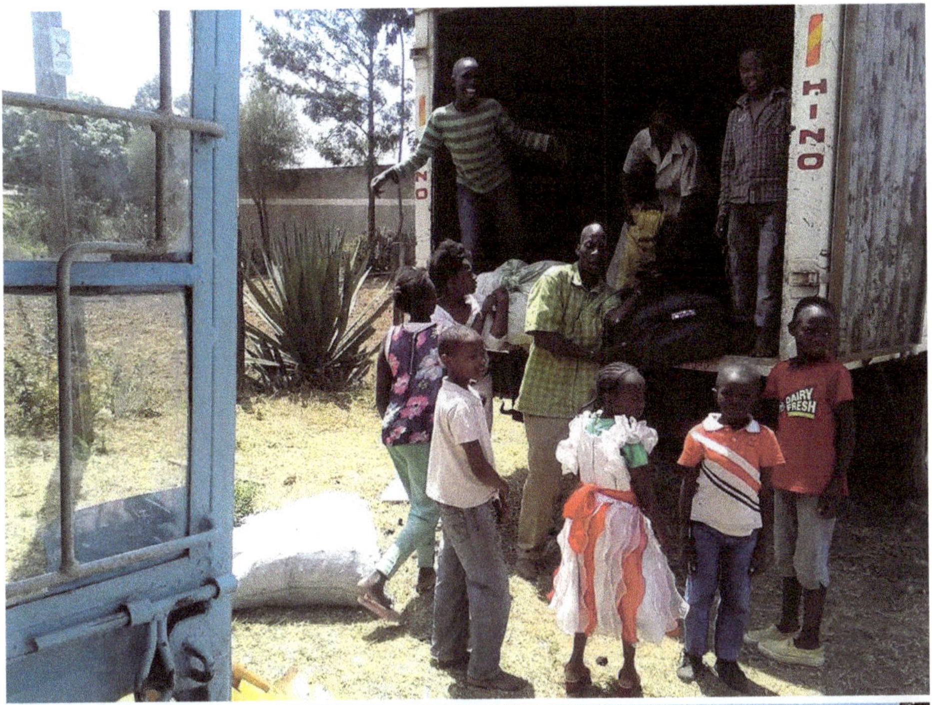

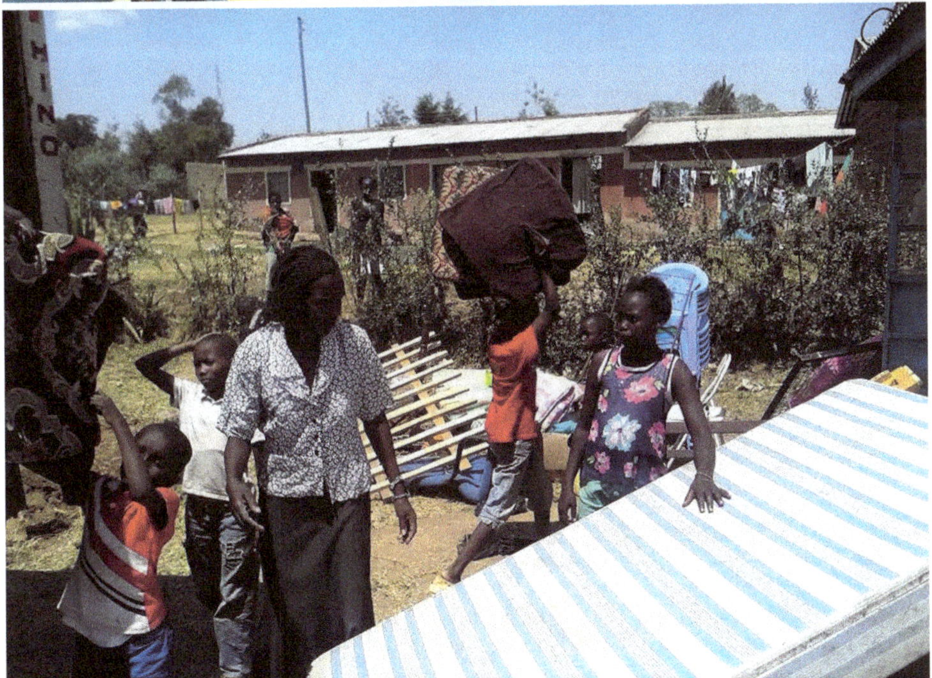

22/06/2018.

Dear friends:

Hello, My name is Jephard Musa; a 7'years old at St Tabitha Othordex ophanage church and School. in Top class.

I respect the people around me and Wishing to go far in my education and become a doctor. Requesting you for more Support

Thank you

Yours sincerely

Jephard Musa.

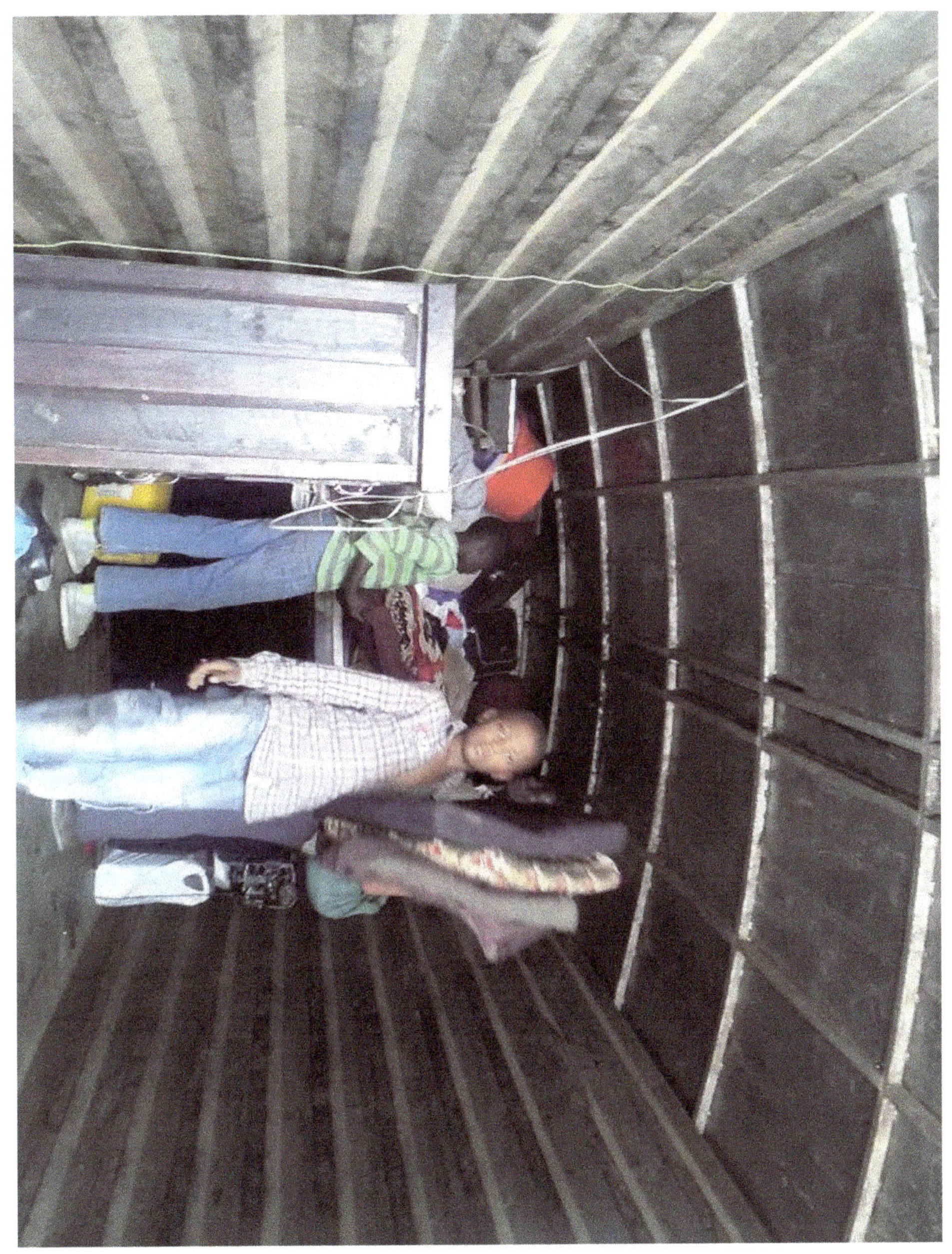

All of the children helped to move everything and they had a lot of fun doing it too.

Everyone was very tired at the end of the day so we all slept well that night.

It is like the Psalm says:
The Lord gives his beloved children sleep.

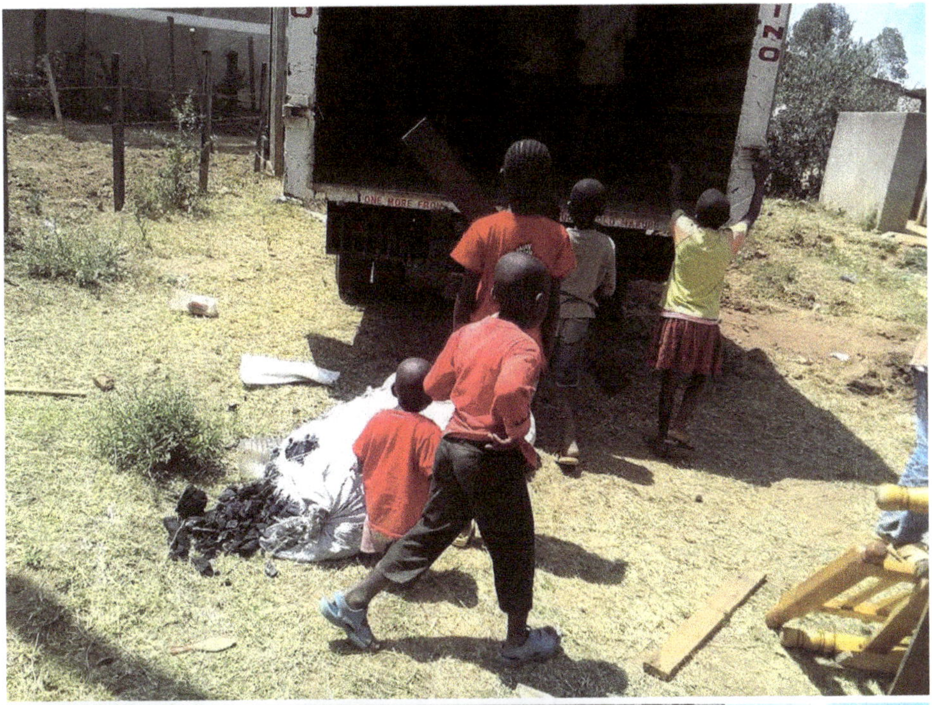

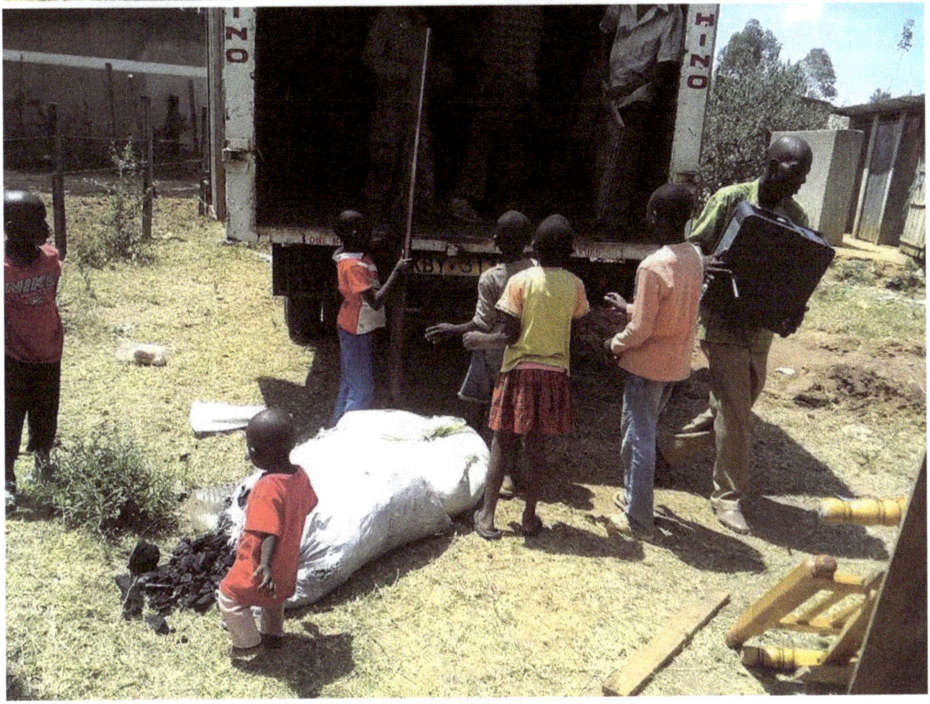

25/4/2018

Dear, friends;

Hello, my name is Mary Nyambura all years-old-girl at ST-Tabitha orthod orphanage church and school in class, 3 I respect. the people around me and wishing togo far in my education and become ateacher. more support Please!

Thank you.

Yours sincerely.

Mary Nyambura.

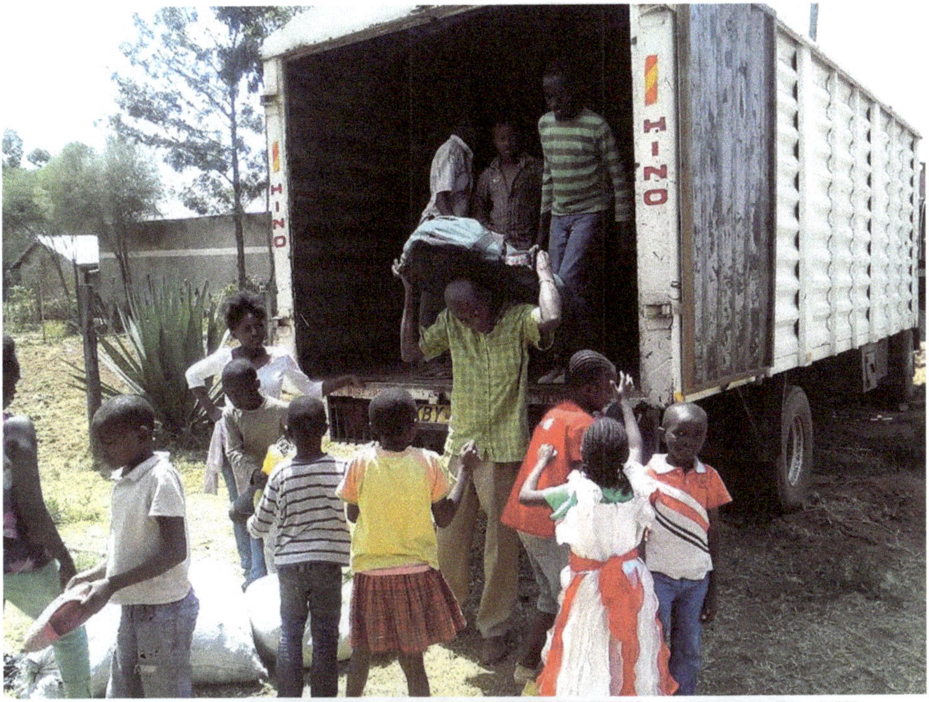

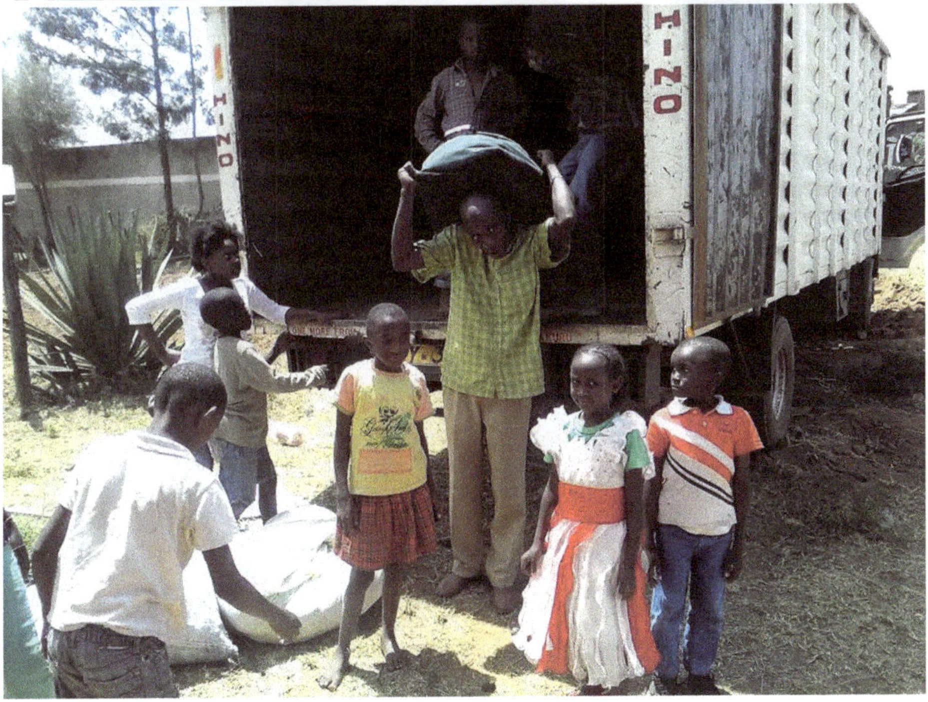

Dear friends.

Hello, my name is Emmanuel nyakundi - 9 9 years old. at St Tabitha othordox ophanage church and school. in class 3.

I respect the people around me and wishing to go far in my education and become a police. man. Requesting you for more support.

Thank you

Yours Sincerely

Emmanuel nyakundi

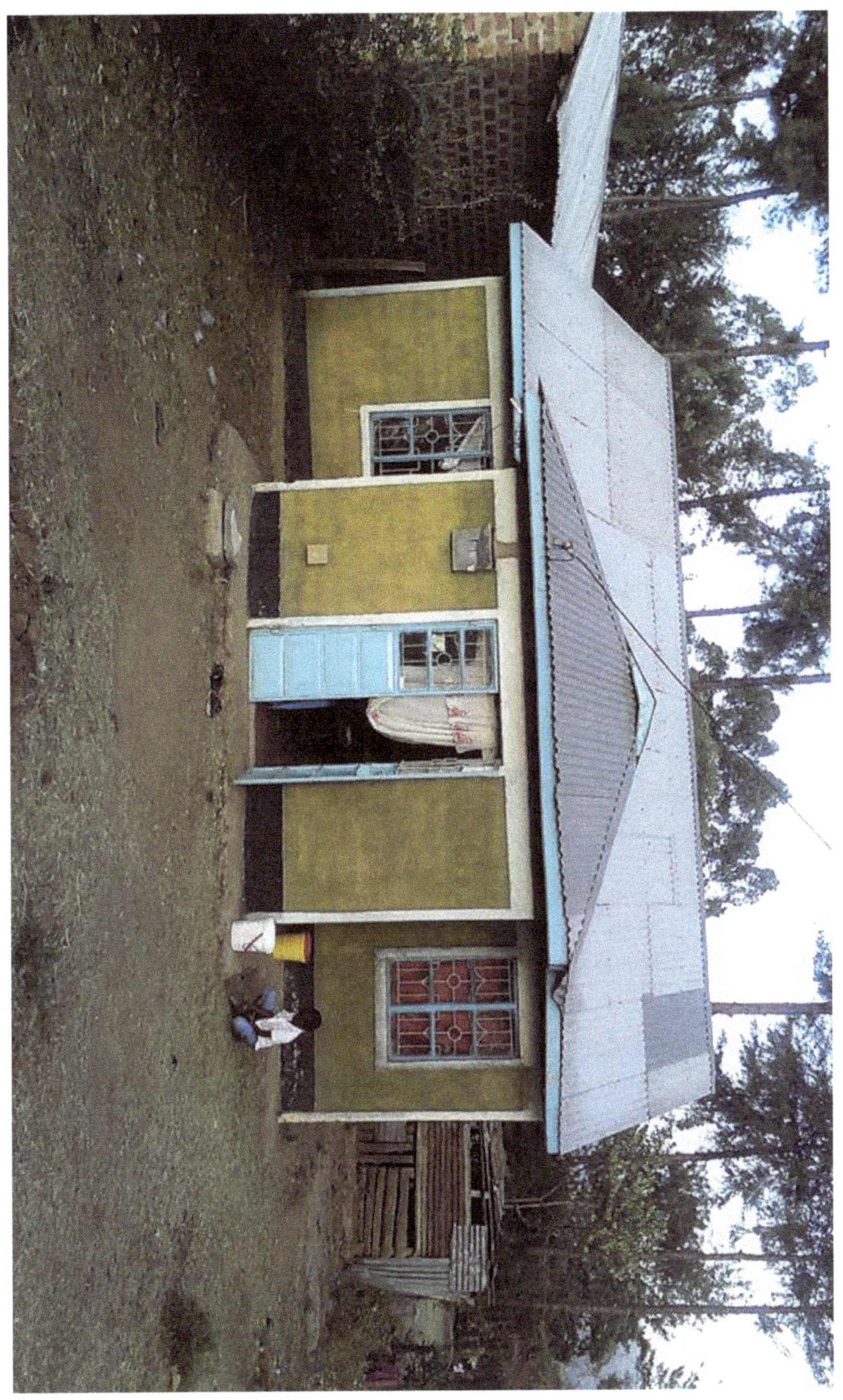

Painting takes a long time and it is a tiring job
but God gives a man the patience to do it.

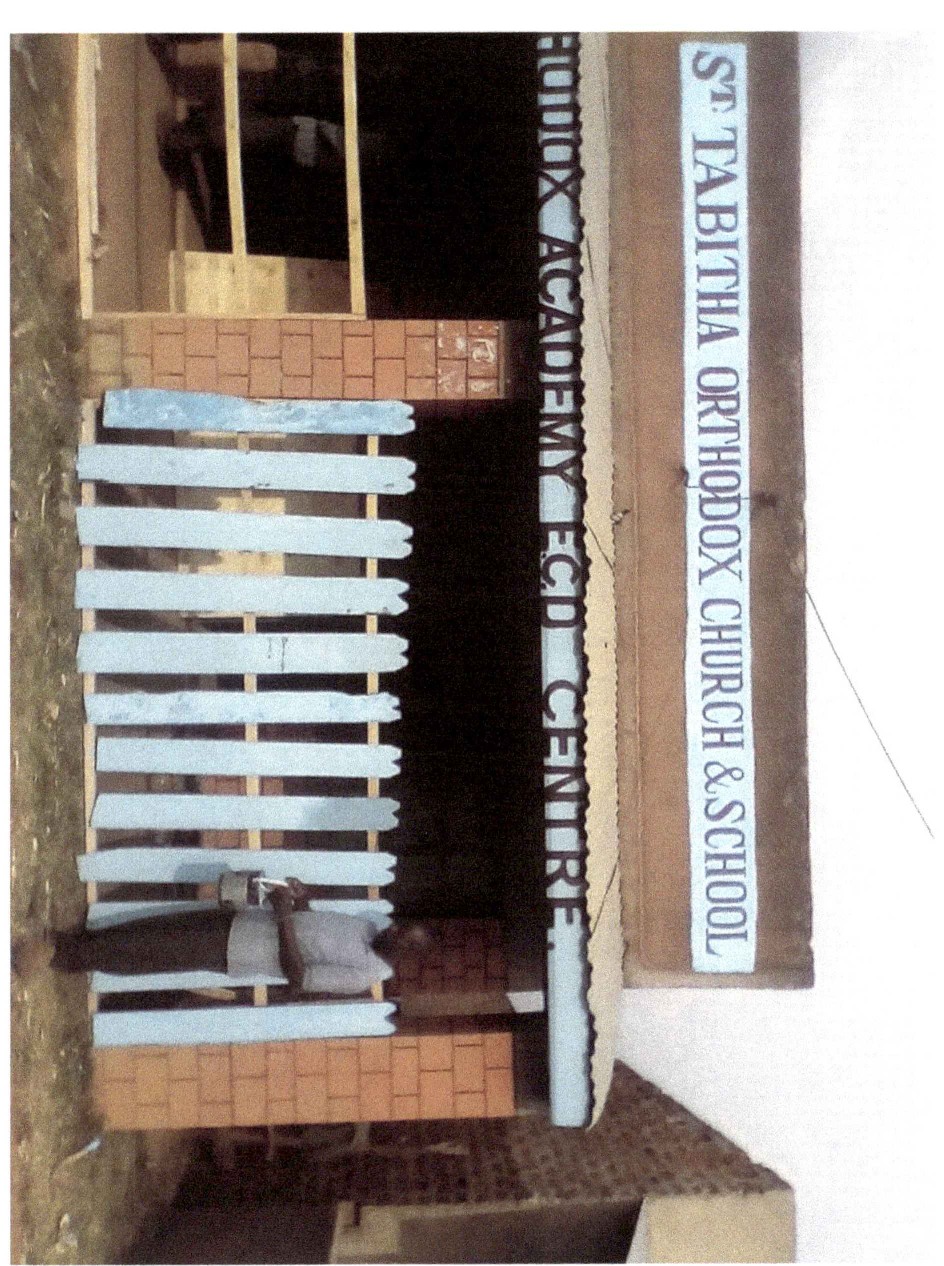
ST. TABITHA ORTHODOX CHURCH & SCHOOL
ACADEMY ECD CENTRE

25-9-2018

Dear friends;

Hello, My name is Faith Andronike Lipesa.
I am 11 years old girl at St Tabitha Orthodox Orphanage church and school in class six.

I scored the following marks in the following Subjects:

1. Math: 72%
2. English 76%
3. Kiswahili 75%
4. Science: 74%
5. Social studies/CRE 71%

But I will put more effort next tearm to score highir marks.

I respect the people around me and wishing to go far in education and became one of the best doctors in the world.

Requesting you for more Support. Thank you.

Yours Sincerely,
Faith Andronike Lipesa

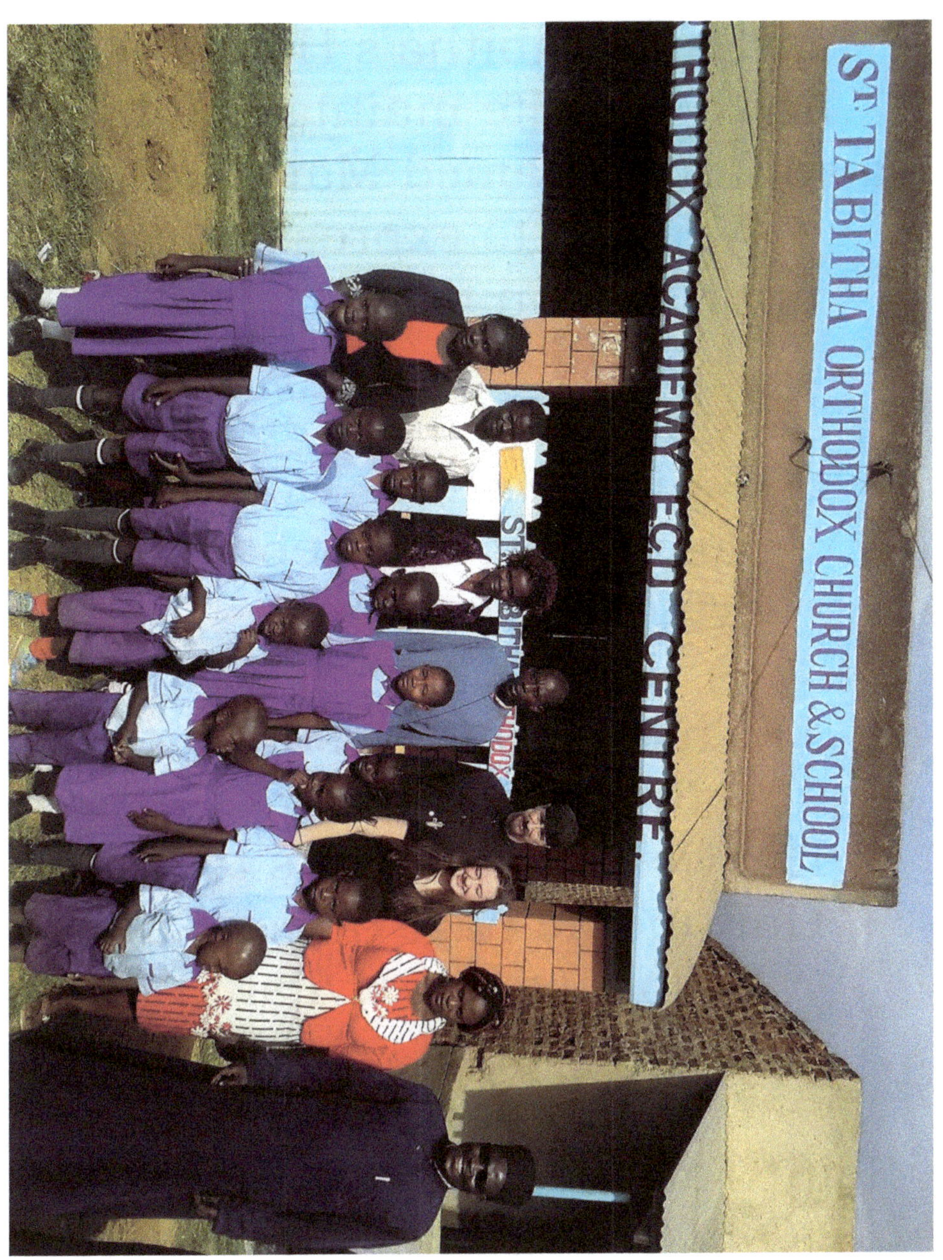
ST TABITHA ORTHODOX CHURCH & SCHOOL
THODOX ACADEMY ECD CENTRE

Saint Tabitha's House
has a website maintained by
a volunteer named Maria Powell.
We wish to express our
appreciation for her efforts.

To find out more about
Saint Tabitha's House
please visit our website:
www.sttabithahouse.com

Please donate to support
this ongoing work.
The website has links to our
GoFundMe page or you can
donate via PayPal.

Write to us at:
Saint Tabitha Community Centre
P.O.BOX 192 Malava, KENYA

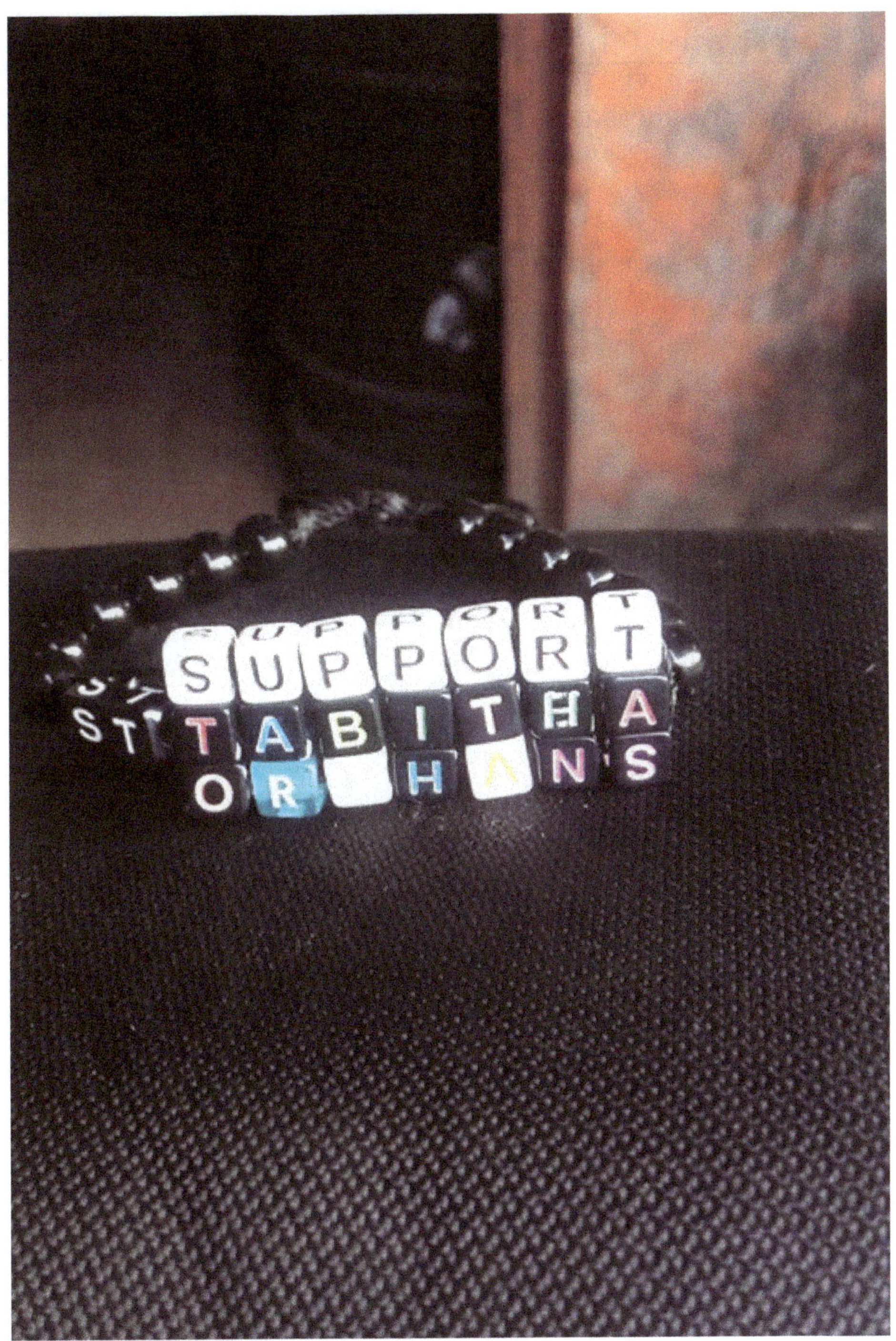
SUPPORT
TABITHA
OR HANS

Play Traitor Chess

by Issachar Saberhagen

Out Now

What if there were traitors on the chessboard? What if the soldiers sometimes followed the orders of the other king? In Traitor Chess, it happens! Lean how to play with this quick guide to the basic rules and some variations.

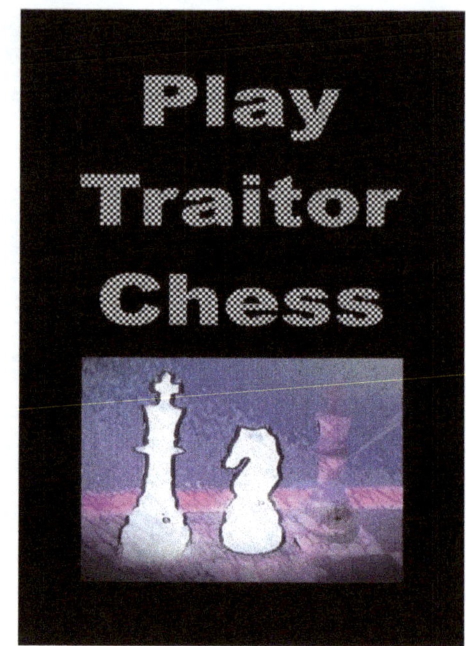

ISBN 9780994179920

Publisher's Future Releases

Foolhardy Words

by Jessy Carlisle

Some poetical insights upon various life issues plus a little gentle advice.

Grandma's Journal

by M. R. Astle

A small collection of memoirs a lady born just before the Great Depression left to her grandson who, with the aid of family, added some photographs and edited the work.

Finding Small One

by Jessy Carlisle

Out Now

Small One is on a search for what's really important in life. But you may be surprised to discover who Small One really is!

ISBN 9780994179906

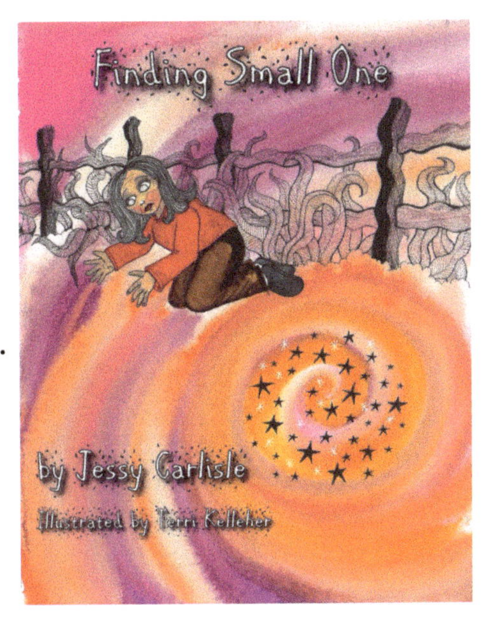

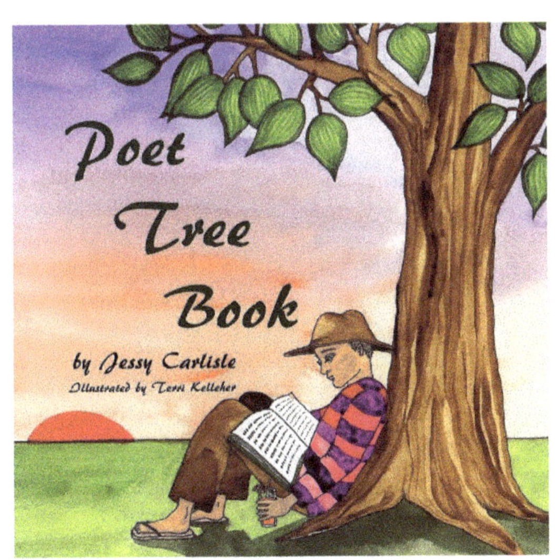

Poet Tree Book

by Jessy Carlisle

Out Now

Australian poet Jessy Carlisle's premier publication including the iconic "I Am a Tree".

ISBN 9780994179913

www.ingramcontent.com/pod-product-compliance
Ingram Content Group UK Ltd.
Pitfield, Milton Keynes, MK11 3LW, UK
UKHW021827270726
14058UKWH00001B/16